PENGUIN BOOKS

CHILDHOOD DAYS

Satyajit Ray was born on 2 May 1921 in Calcutta. After graduating from Presidency College, Calcutta, in 1940, he studied art at Rabindranath Tagore's university, Shantiniketan. By 1943, Ray was back in Calcutta and had joined an advertising firm as a visualizer. He also started designing covers and illustrating books brought out by Signet Press. A deep interest in films led to his establishing the Calcutta Film Society in 1947. During a six-month trip to Europe, in 1950, Ray became a member of the London Film Club and managed to see ninety-nine films in only four-and-a-half months.

In 1955, after overcoming innumerable difficulties, Satyajit Ray completed his first film, *Pather Panchali*, with financial assistance from the West Bengal government. The film was an award-winner at the Cannes Film Festival and established Ray as a director of international stature. Together with *Aparajito* (The Unvanquished, 1956) and *Apur Sansar* (The World of Apu, 1959), it forms the Apu trilogy and perhaps constitutes Ray's finest work. Ray's other films include *Jalsaghar* (The Music Room, 1958), *Charulata* (1964), *Aranyer Din Ratri* (Days and Nights in the Forest, 1970), *Shatranj Ke Khilari* (The Chess Players, 1977), *Ghare Baire* (The Home and the World, 1984), *Ganashatru* (Enemy of the People, 1989), *Shakha Proshakha* (Branches of a Tree, 1990), and *Agantuk* (The Stranger, 1991). Ray also made several documentaries, including one on Tagore. In 1987, he made the documentary *Sukumar Ray*, to commemorate the birth centenary of his father, perhaps Bengal's most famous writer of nonsense verse and children's books. Satyajit Ray won numerous awards for his films. Both the British Federation of Film Societies and the Moscow Film Festival Committee named him one of the greatest directors of the second half of the twentieth century. In 1992, he was awarded the Oscar for Lifetime Achievement by the Academy of Motion Picture Arts and Science and, in the same year, was also honoured with the Bharat Ratna.

Apart from being a film-maker, Satyajit Ray was a writer of repute. In 1961, he revived the children's magazine, *Sandesh*, which his grandfather, Upendra Kishore Ray, had started and to which his father used to contribute frequently. Satyajit Ray contributed numerous poems, stories and essays to *Sandesh*, and also published several novels in Bengali, most of which became best-sellers. In 1978, Oxford University awarded him its D.Litt degree.

Satyajit Ray died in Calcutta in April 1992.

*

Bijoya Ray was born in 1918 and spent the first thirteen years of her life in Patna where her father worked as a barrister. She moved to Calcutta in 1931 along with her family, where she and Satyajit Ray happened to stay in the same house. She went on to become an accomplished singer and recorded her songs with Hindustan Records. After graduating, she joined the Bengali film industry and also went to Bombay. It was while she was in Bombay, in 1948, that she got married to Satyajit Ray. When Ray revived *Sandesh* in 1961, Bijoya became an occasional contributor. After her husband's death in 1992, she has become one of the editors of *Sandesh*, and has also written for other eminent Bengali journals.

Bijoya Ray lives in Calcutta with her son, Sandip.

Satyajit Ray

Childhood Days
A Memoir

Translated from the Bengali by
Bijoya Ray

PENGUIN BOOKS

PENGUIN BOOKS

Published by the Penguin Group

Penguin Books India Pvt. Ltd, 11 Community Centre, Panchsheel Park, New Delhi 110 017, India

Penguin Group (USA) Inc., 375 Hudson Street, New York, New York 10014, USA

Penguin Group (Canada), 90 Eglinton Avenue East, Suite 700, Toronto, Ontario, M4P 2Y3, Canada (a division of Pearson Penguin Canada Inc.)

Penguin Books Ltd, 80 Strand, London WC2R 0RL, England

Penguin Ireland, 25 St Stephen's Green, Dublin 2, Ireland (a division of Penguin Books Ltd)

Penguin Group (Australia), 250 Camberwell Road, Camberwell, Victoria 3124, Australia (a division of Pearson Australia Group Pty Ltd)

Penguin Group (NZ), 67 Apollo Drive, Rosedale, North Shore 0632, New Zealand (a division of Pearson New Zealand Ltd)

Penguin Group (South Africa) (Pty) Ltd, 24 Sturdee Avenue, Rosebank, Johannesburg 2196, South Africa

Penguin Books Ltd, Registered Offices: 80 Strand, London WC2R 0RL, England

Childhood Days first appeared serially in Sandesh in 1980, 1981. It was first published in book form in Bengali by Ananda Publishers, Calcutta in 1982. Making Movies was first published in Bengali by Neuscript, Calcutta in 1979; this translation is from the revised edition published by Ananda Publishers, Calcutta in 1988. The following stories in Making Movies first appeared in Bengali in Sandesh: 'Two and half years with Apu' (1982), 'Project Tiger' (1976), 'Hundi-Jhundi-Shundi' (1977), 'The Army of Raja of Halla' (1976), 'Camels Versus Trains' (1975), 'With Feluda in Varanasi' (1978), 'Please, Please Bagh Mama' (1981).

15 14 13 12

ISBN 9780140250794

Typeset in Times Roman by Digital Technologies and Printing Solutions, New Delhi
Printed at Yash Printographics, Noida

Contents

Contents

Anyone even remotely familiar with my husband's work, or his personality, would know that he aroused not just curiosity in people, but a feeling of awe. Perhaps that is how every celebrity appears to those who admire him—a figure larger than life, almost unreal in its immensity.

Those who knew him well, however, were aware that he was, in fact, just the opposite of how he might have appeared. The man who towered over everyone else, not only in physical height but in every other sense, quite possibly seemed remote and aloof to outsiders. To his family and friends, he was no different from other normal men—warm, affectionate, hospitable, helpful and as willing to have a laugh as anyone else. Many of those who knew and worked with him closely have told me that what they remember most about him is his smile, and the booming laughter he often broke into when he was amused.

Considering his lineage, it is hardly surprising that Manik should have been blessed with a fine sense of humour and a warm, positive approach to life. It would have been surprising if the grandson of Upendra Kishore and the son of Sukumar Ray had *not* turned out to be a humanist. His films bear enough evidence of his concern and sympathy for people. But it was when he began writing for the *Sandesh* magazine for children, which he revived in 1961, that I think he became closer to his admirers. Even if adults still revered him from afar, their children had no hesitation in hailing Manik as a friend, one who understood their joys and sorrows, and could be relied upon to remain on their side at all times.

It was for this reason that the curiosity regarding Manik's own childhood grew steadily. Usually, Manik did not like talking about himself. If anyone asked him direct questions, he answered them, but confined himself to facts. So everyone learnt about when and where he was born, where he lived, and which school he went to. This did not, however, tell anyone about what he did as a child, what he thought, who he played with, what was his family like, what interested him, and how the seeds were sown in his early life that made him the man he was.

Childhood Days (*Jokhon Chhoto Chhilam*), serialized in *Sandesh*, answered these questions. It was the only piece of his writing in which he spoke about himself and his family. It is not difficult to see why these brief accounts came to be so widely read. The readers of *Sandesh*, for whom the memoirs were chiefly intended, were delighted to discover that the famous editor of their magazine, the creator of the legendary Feluda and Shonku, had been a normal, happy child, no different from themselves. Like them, he had been puzzled at times by the behaviour of adults, but had learnt not to question them. Like many children, he too had to face teachers of whom he was afraid: and when it came to his classmates, he had to put up with endless teasing, for no one spared him just because he came from a distinguished background. To the adults who read them, these memoirs provided an insight into the mind of the celebrated film-maker and writer, his ideas and beliefs that took shape during his formative years. For those who wanted to produce articles and books on Satyajit Ray, *Jokhon Chhoto Chhilam* became a vital point of reference.

Soon after its publication, Manik began to receive from

various people, both in India and abroad, offers to translate the
whole collection into English. Some even went to the extent of
actually doing it and sending it to Manik, apparently confident
that he would be flattered into giving his permission for its
publication. Had the quality of any of these translations been
acceptable, he might well have considered giving his approval.
Sadly, such was not the case. Yet, it was obvious both to Manik
and myself that if the collection could be translated properly,
there was a much wider audience that would welcome it with
open arms.

Eventually, Manik decided to translate it himself. But the
pressure of film-making and his own failing health made it
impossible. When he passed away in 1992, for a long time I did
not think of his childhood memoirs at all. I was then working
on the manuscript of *My Years with Apu*, trying to salvage
something out of a rough draft that he had left behind. When
that was done, it occurred to me one day that perhaps now was
the time to do something about *Childhood Days*. I knew, better
than anyone else, how much it had meant to Manik. To be
honest, it meant a lot to me, too, because it spoke of a time I
had lived in; it spoke of people I had known. For this reason,
instead of passing it on to anyone else, I decided to take on the
job of translating *Childhood Days* myself.

Perhaps it is not generally known that Manik and I had
grown up together. There are many childhood memories that
we shared. He has related some of these; others I still cherish
in my heart. Leafing through the pages of this book and reading
about his earliest memories, my mind often goes back to a
particular incident when we were both small. Let me tell you
about it.

Manik came to our house in Patna for a visit. One day, one
of our aunts (the singer, Kanak Biswas) suggested a drawing
competition between him and me. This came about, I think,

because I had stood first in my drawing class that year. Manik being younger, I thought rather smugly that the prize would definitely come to me. We were both given a picture to copy. Even now, I can remember every detail of that picture. It showed a well-dressed young girl about to feed a parrot in a cage. Her hair was tied back with a ribbon and in one hand she held a doll. When we finished copying it, everyone praised my efforts. But when my own mother saw Manik's drawing, she said without a moment's hesitation, 'I think the prize must go to Manik.' At this, I promptly burst into tears. 'Don't cry,' my mother said. 'Just look at this picture. See for yourself how well Manik has drawn.' Still weeping, I raised my face and looked at his picture. My tears dried instantly. Truly, it was far better than mine. I had used an eraser many times. My picture was therefore somewhat untidy. Manik had not used an eraser even once. His strokes were so clear that, for a moment, it seemed as if his drawing was even better than the original! There was so longer any doubt in my mind about who deserved the prize. Manik was then only five years old.

In his book, Manik mentions Kanak Biswas, and describes how nervous she got when she went to record her first song. It is an amusing tale, but every time I read it, I am reminded of my own nervousness in a recording studio. Music has been a passion for me ever since I can remember. In fact, it was our interest in music that drew Manik and me closer together. As a young woman, I, too, had recorded a number of songs. Yet, each time, just before the recording began, my throat invariably went totally dry, and my vocal cords seemed to disappear. Manik may have been amused by our aunt's plight, but I can feel a lot of sympathy for her.

Once I had begun working on *Childhood Days*, something else occurred to me. There was a second book, called *Ekei Bauley Shooting* (Making Movies) which was another collection of reminiscences, also published in *Sandesh* before it was released as a book. In it, Manik related some of his experiences while shooting *Pather Panchali* (The Song of the Road); the two films featuring Goopy and Bagha; and the famous Feluda films. Here, he spoke as a film-maker, offering his young readers a glimpse of the world he lived in. Until these accounts were published, I doubt if many people knew just how much effort went into making a film, how much planning had to be done, and how quick and clever a director had to be when unforeseen problems cropped up. I felt sure that if these tales could be included, the readers would be happy to find an additional bonus.

For me, personally, these accounts once again brought back many fond memories. After all, I had made the same journey with Manik, from the days of looking desperately for a young boy to play Apu, to travelling in Rajasthan with Feluda and his team. I had been there when they caught Maganlal in Varanasi; and I had watched Goopy and Bagha struggling to get past a tiger in *Hirak Rajar Deshey* (The Kingdom of Diamonds). I knew I would enjoy translating *Making Movies* as much as *Childhood Days*.

So I began with a lot of enthusiasm, but ill-health started to interfere with my work, forcing me to stop frequently for long periods. It took me more than a year to finish these books. When I did, I passed both manuscripts to Penguin with a mixture of pleasure and relief. Unfortunately, my health did not improve; so when it came to working together with the editor of Penguin to give the whole book its final shape, I found myself unable to do what was required of me. How much longer the project would have been delayed, it is difficult to tell. But, last year, two things happened by a happy coincidence. Gopa Majumdar finished translating all the Feluda stories, a mammoth task she had undertaken five years ago, and Penguin India acquired a

new editor called Sudeshna Shome Ghosh, who was familiar
with the original text. At my request, Gopa and Sudeshna got
together and handled all the editorial tasks swiftly and skilfully.
I am very grateful to both of them for their help. My sincere
thanks also go to David Davidar of Penguin for his unfailing
patience and support.

It is, naturally, for the reader to judge how the finished
product stands. For my part, I think Manik would have been
pleased.

Calcutta   Bijoya Ray
October 1998

THE RAY FAMILY TREE (PATERNAL SIDE)

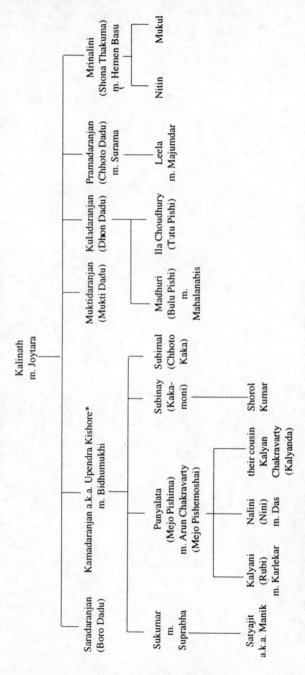

* A zamindar, lawyer and relative of the Ray family, Harikishore Ray Choudhury had adopted Kamadaranjan and had renamed him Upendra Kishore.

THE RAY FAMILY TREE (MATERNAL SIDE)

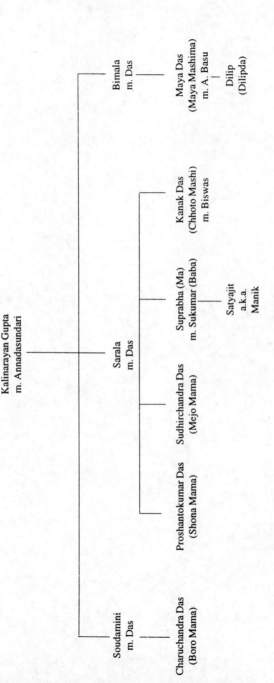

Kalinarayan Gupta
m. Annadasundari

Soudamini
m. Das

Charuchandra Das
(Boro Mama)

Sarala
m. Das

Proshantokumar Das
(Shona Mama)

Sudhirchandra Das
(Mejo Mama)

Suprabha (Ma)
m. Sukumar (Baba)

Satyajit
a.k.a.
Manik

Kanak Das
(Chhoto Mashi)
m. Biswas

Bimala
m. Das

Maya Das
(Maya Mashima)
m. A. Basu

Dilip
(Dilipda)

Courtesy: Indrani Majumdar

Childhood Days

Illustrations by Satyajit Ray

Introduction

It is impossible to tell which bits of one's memories of childhood would remain for ever, and which would disappear without a trace. There is no hard and fast rule that governs the function of memory. That is what makes it such a mysterious business. I was five years old when we left the house in Gorpar where I was born, and moved to Bhowanipur. I cannot recall anything of the day when we actually left the old house, but I remember a dream I had one night while we were still living there. It featured our cook's son, Haren, but there was nothing remarkable about the dream. Yet, I remember every little detail.

In these childhood memoirs I have described some ordinary events and ordinary people, as well as extraordinary ones. Children do not make a distinction between the ordinary and the extraordinary, anyway. Adults do. It is for this reason that children do not pick and choose their friends like adults; nor do they understand or always obey the criteria laid down by grown-ups.

These memoirs were first published in the monthly magazine *Sandesh* in two instalments. Later, I was able to recall a few more events and some more people from my childhood, so I added them here.

So many things from my childhood have now disappeared altogether. Does anyone ever see signs saying 'To Let' nowadays, hanging from balconies of houses? In those days they were a common sight everywhere. Then there were the open-topped red double-decker buses run by the Wallford Company. There was a special charm in travelling on the top deck of these buses, feeling the wind play on one's face and hair. The roads were far less crowded, and the menace of traffic jams almost unheard of. But the biggest difference with the roads of today, I think, was in the appearance of the motor cars. Heaven knows how many different makes from different countries ran on the streets of Calcutta. Each car had a distinctive look, as well as a distinctive horn. It was possible to identify a car by the sound of its horn. There were Fords, Chevrolets, Humbers, Vauxhalls, Wolseleys, Dodges, Buicks, Austins, Studebakers, Morrises, Oldsmobiles, Opels, Citroens . . . all these have vanished completely from the city. So have open-hood convertibles. Only rarely does one get to see baby Austins or the huge Lancia and Lassel with their 'boa horns', which were shaped like a snake's mouth. These majestic cars have faded away into a dream. Then came the first streamlined cars, looking a bit like tortoise shells, but even that was a very long time ago.

Another thing that has disappeared is horse-drawn carriages. When we lived in Gorpar, we did not have a car. So we often rode in these carriages. Box carriages were never comfortable, but I remember rides in phaetons, which I enjoyed.

The sound of jet planes thundering across the sky—now so common—was almost totally unknown in those days. Only occasionally did we get to see one or two two-seater planes. The Dum Dum and Behala flying clubs had only just started, and Bengalis were learning to fly. Planes were used to scatter handbills in the city, in thousands at a time. They came floating down from the sky and settled in various corners of the city. Once, some of them fell on the roof of our house. I picked them up and found they were advertisements for the Bata shoe company.

An amazing number of ordinary everyday things have changed so much over the years. In the days before the advent of nylon, we used white Kolynos toothbrushes and Kolynos toothpaste. We had black-coloured Swan and Waterman fountain pens, made of something called guttapercha. If burnt, it gave out a most unpleasant smell. But I have to admit those pens lasted far longer than pens do today.

In this age of Kwality and Farrini, who bothers to make ice cream at home? But in our time, vanilla ice cream was often made at home in a wooden bucket which had an iron handle fixed to it. The sound of this handle being turned to churn the ice cream always made my heart dance with joy. The taste of home-made ice cream was always so much better than the ones we could buy from push-carts on the streets.

Illnesses in my childhood meant a bottle of mixture that the chemist made up from the doctor's prescription. A white label used to be stuck on one side of the bottle with each measure marked out. I found this most intriguing. For a common cold, a warm footbath was often recommended. It meant sitting with one's feet soaking in a tub of hot water, after making sure all doors and windows were firmly shut. What I cannot remember now is whether this helped in any way to cure the cold. In those days, the only laxative we had was castor oil, which made me want to throw up. There was nothing but quinine pills for the treatment of malaria. As a child, I could not swallow pills whole. Once, before a visit to Dhaka, I was obliged to chew some quinine pills. Even after all these years, I can feel its horrible bitter taste lingering in my mouth. The arrival of capsules in our lives has made us forget how awful the taste of medicines can be.

*

One does not usually remember things from one's early childhood. When my father died, I was only two and a half years old. I cannot seem to recall anything about the tragedy that befell us. But I do have memories of two events that took place when he was ailing. I could not have been more than two years old at the time.

My father fell ill soon after I was born. He never recovered; but occasionally, if he happened to be feeling a little better, he was taken out of Calcutta for a change of air. I remember going to Sodhpur and Giridih with him. The house in Sodhpur was by the Ganges, and it had a courtyard. One day my father was sitting by the window and painting, when I suddenly heard him say, 'There's a ship!' I ran out into the courtyard and saw a steamer pass by, hooting loudly.

In my memories of Giridih, our old servant Prayag features, not my father. Prayag and I were sitting on the sandy bank of the river Usri one evening, when he said, 'If you dig the sand, you'll find water.' Much excited, I began digging with a wooden spade someone had bought me from a toyshop. After a while, water did trickle out of the sand; but, at that precise moment, a girl from a nearby village appeared out of nowhere

and calmly washed her hands in our water! I remember feeling distinctly annoyed by someone else washing their hands in the water that we had found.

*

I was born in 100, Gorpar Road in Calcutta, and lived there until I was five. Since then, I have lived in many houses, all in south Calcutta, but never in a house as remarkable as the one in which I was born.

It was not just a house, but a printing press as well. My grandfather, Upendra Kishore, had designed the house himself, but was able to live in it for just four years. He died five and a half years before I was born. High on the wall in front of our house, 'U RAY & SONS, PRINTERS AND BLOCK MAKERS', was written in large letters. To get to the press, one had to pass through the gate, go past chowkidar Hanuman Mishir's room and up a flight of steps. A huge door marked the entrance to the press. The press was on the ground floor; the rooms for block-making and typesetting were directly above it, on the first floor. We lived in the rear of the house. A little lane to the left led to the entrance door of the residential portion of the house. The door opened to a flight of stairs. Those who had business in the press, turned left as they came up the stairs; and our friends and relatives turned right to go into the portion where we lived. The door on the left led to the block-making department, and the one on the right led to our drawing room.

Right next to our house, on the western side, was a school for the deaf and dumb. On the eastern side, opposite our garden wall, stood the Athenaeum Institution. In the rather eerie silence of the afternoon, when the noise of the traffic ceased, we could hear the students at the institution chant multiplication tables and read aloud from their books. This was followed sometimes by rebukes from irate masters. In the evening, the pupils of this school used to come out and play in their sports ground, which was visible from our roof. The main event worth watching was their annual sports day.

The roof was where we played blindman's buff. We also flew kites from there. My grandfather's study was on the second floor. I had always seen it empty. One of its contents, in the course of time, became my own property. It was a wooden box in which my grandfather used to keep his paints, brushes and bottles of linseed oil.

Several other people lived in that house, apart from my mother and myself. They were my father's younger brothers, Subinay and Subimal Ray; my great-uncle (Upendra Kishore's brother) Kuladaranjan; and my grandmother.

Subinay lived on the second floor. I called him Kakamoni. It was he who took charge of the press when my father died. Paper samples of various kinds often arrived from Germany in those days. Thick, thin, silky, shiny, rough or coarse—there was no end to their variety. If I went into Kakamoni's room, he used to hand me a book of samples and say, 'Take a look and tell me which one we should order.' I would then feel the surface of each sample, as if I was an expert, and declare my views, convinced that my uncle would order from Germany only what I had chosen.

Kakamoni's son, Shorol, was the only cousin on my father's side. He and his mother stayed in Jabalpur most of the time with his mother's family. He went to an English-medium school there. The English boys in his school called him Cyril.

Subimal Ray, my Chhoto Kaka, also lived on the second floor. I came to spend a lot of time with him much later in life. The only thing I remember about him from when we lived in Gorpar is that he always took at least an hour more than the rest of us to finish a meal. This was because he felt he had to chew every mouthful thirty-two times, or nothing he ate would ever get digested.

My mother and I had a room on the first floor, just below Kakamoni's. My widowed grandmother lived on the same floor. I spent long hours with her sorting out and cleaning old picture-blocks that had once been used for *Sandesh*. She died before we left Gorpar.

The person I remember most clearly from among those who lived in the Gorpar house was my greatuncle, Kuladaranjan—Dhon Dadu to me. His room was on the ground floor, directly below ours. Dadu spent his time lifting heavy clubs, enlarging photos of dead people, telling me stories from Indian mythology and taking an avid interest in cricket. By the time I got to know him, he was too old to play. But I heard, more than once, of his past experiences in the cricket ground. Once, while playing for the Bengali team at the Town Club against an awesome English team, he got stuck at ninety-nine. He loved describing how he eventually scored a century after many anxious moments. When the MCC or the Australian cricket team visited Calcutta, Dadu could think of nothing but Eden Gardens.

His main occupation was enlarging photographs. He carried out the entire process including the finishing on the photographs in his own room. I used to stand there and watch him. He had an easel—the kind that is used for oil paintings—on which he placed the enlarged photograph. Then he pressed with his foot what looked like a pair of bellows, and holding a nozzle in his hand, sprayed colour on the photo to add the final finishing touches. Most photos ended up black or dark brown, but on one occasion, I remember he was able to bring out the green in the surrounding plants and the red in the Kashmiri shawl the subject was wearing. It was a photo of the Maharaja of Nator, Jagadeendra Narayan. I can also remember the new maharaja, Jogeendra Narayan, sitting with me and watching the whole process.

If anybody died from our immediate circle of friends, Dadu was requested to enlarge the dead person's photo. It was often no more than a small face in an old and hazy group photo. Yet, when Dadu produced the finished product, it always seemed as if the real person was staring out of the frame. Dadu would be seen, within a few days of the death, with a brown paper packet under his arms. When the photograph was unveiled and displayed, close family and friends of the dead person were so moved that they were often found wiping their tears. I myself saw this happen several times.

Dadu also wrote for children. U Ray & Sons published many of his stories before we left Gorpar: the *Iliad*, the *Odyssey*, legends and fables, the *Twenty-five Betaal Stories*, *Thirty-two Simhasan Stories* and the *Kathasaritsagar*. These books used to be kept in piles behind a partition. Most of the stories had already been published in *Sandesh*.

Sandesh continued to be published for two years after my father's death. I can still remember it being printed in our press with its cover of three different colours. I usually visited the press in the afternoon. The first thing one saw on entering were the compositors who sat in rows, bent over their type-cases with different compartments, picking out letters and arranging them in rows to match the text. Their faces soon became familiar to me. All of them would look up and smile at me when I made an appearance. I used to walk past them and go to the back of the room. Even now, every time I smell turpentine oil, an image of the block-making department of U Ray & Sons rises before my eyes. In the middle of the room stood the huge process camera. One man had learnt to handle it extremely well. It was Ramdaheen. He came from Bihar, and had originally started work as a mere bearer. My grandfather had taught him how to operate the camera. Ramdaheen was like a family member, so I thrust all my little demands upon him. I would pick up a piece of paper, draw funny squiggles on it and pass it to him. 'This must come out in *Sandesh*,' I would say. Ramdaheen would nod vigorously and reply, 'Yes, Khokababu, yes!' Then he'd place my drawing under the lens of the camera, pick me up in his arms and show me the upside-down image of it through the glazed glass behind the camera.

I cannot recall much about studies and lessons in Gorpar. There are some faint memories of an aunt called Bulu Pishi giving me lessons in English. The book she read out from was called *Step by Step*. I can even vaguely recall what the book looked like. My mother must have taught me too, but I don't remember taking lessons from her. What I do remember is her reading stories from an English book and retelling them in Bengali. Two of these were horror stories that I never forgot: Conan Doyle's 'Blue John Gap' and 'The Brazilian Cat'.

Bulu Pishi had a sister called Tutu, who lived in Upper Circular Road, which was just a three-minute walk from our house. If anyone in our house happened to fall ill, my mother always took charge of nursing that person. Whenever this happened, I was sent off to stay with Tutu Pishi. I loved the house she lived in with its red mosaic floor and colourful windowpanes. Its front veranda overlooked the main road, by the side of which was a railway line. Only small freight trains ran on that line, usually carrying all the rubbish from the city to a waste disposal ground called Dhapa. People jokingly referred to the train as the 'Dhapa Mail'.

Tutu Pishi herself took charge of my studies during the time I spent with her. Her husband often took me for a drive in the evening after he returned from work. I used to go back to my own house in Gorpar as soon as the ailing patient recovered.

Sometimes, we used to visit the house of Sir Jagadish Bose. He also lived in Upper Circular Road, only a short distance away. Jagadish Bose was a very famous scientist, having proved that plants have life, and had received a knighthood for this. However, we went to his house not to look at him, but to see the little zoo he had by the side of his garden.

Most of my evenings were spent on the roof of our house in Gorpar.

I had no siblings, but did not lack playmates. Our cook's son, Haren, was the same age as me. There was also Chhedi, whose mother Shyama was one of our maids. Chhedi was older by about five years. Shyama came from Motihari in Bihar. Although she could speak broken Bengali, sometimes—if taken aback by something—her hand would fly to her cheek and she would burst into her own dialect.

Chhedi had learnt to speak fluent Bengali. Among his many talents was his expertise in flying kites. The thread attached to a kite had to be plastered with manja, which was a concoction of fine powdered glass and glue. This was done on the roof, simply by winding the thread around three iron pillars. My special job was to hold the reel. On the day of Vishwakarma puja, when virtually everyone in Calcutta flew kites, Chhedi's talent found its fullest expression. The sky rang with shouts from neighbouring houses: 'Duyokko!' (Shame, shame!), 'Parenakko!' (Can't do it!). These were challenges thrown out to rival kite-fliers. Each time a thread was cut and a kite captured, jubilant voices cried, 'Bhokatta!' (Your kite's gone!).

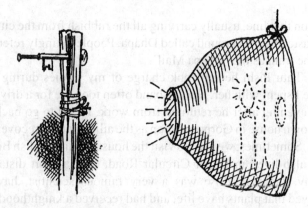

It was not just kites Chhedi was good at making. He was really very good with his hands. From the age of ten, he had begun to make hot air balloons from coloured tissue paper, which we flew from our roof on Kali puja. Apart from this, Chhedi made two things, when I have never seen anywhere else.

One of these was a key-banger. Taking a bamboo the length of his arm, he split its top end slightly and inserted the handle of a key in such a way that its point stuck out at a right angle. It always had to be a key with a little hole at its pointed end, for the hole had to be filled with gunpowder. Chhedi scraped off the gunpowder from matchsticks and poured it into the key. Then he placed a tight-fitting nail into the hole, making sure a gap of about an inch remained between the gunpowder at the bottom and the tip of the nail. Having done this, he would hold the bamboo firmly in one hand and strike the head of the nail sharply against a wall. The compressed air inside the key made the gunpowder go off, making a noise nearly as loud as a real bomb.

The second extraordinary object Chhedi created was a kind of lantern from an empty pot of yoghurt. I found this absolutely fascinating. He would take the clay pot and remove the circular bit from its bottom, closing the gap with a piece of coloured glass. Then he would lay the pot on its side, set up a candle in it and light it, covering the mouth of the pot with a piece of cardboard. The cardboard had a hole in it, which was necessary to let air in, or the candle would go out.

Finally, Chhedi tied a string round the edge of the pot and, holding it in his hand, moved in the dark. A warm, colourful glow shone out of the pot, making it look like a very attractive lantern.

*

My grandfather had four brothers. All but two of the brothers had become members of the Brahmo Samaj. The two who had remained Hindus were Saradaranjan and Muktidaranjan. The women in their houses wore sindoor in the parting of their hair, wrapped their sarees in a different way, and the men had amulets on their arms. The sound of bells and conch shells rang out from their puja rooms, and my aunts often fed me prasad at the end of a puja. None of this happened in my own home, but that never made me feel like an alien in their Hindu households. To tell the truth, the only difference between my grandfather and his brothers seemed to be religion. Their other interests in life were very similar. The Hindu brothers were as passionate about sports—including fishing—as the Brahmos. It was Saradaranjan who started playing cricket before anyone else, and gradually, almost everyone in the family took it up.

But it was really in the family of their sister that cricket took firm root. I called my grandfather's sister Shona Thakuma. She was married to a man called Hemen Bose, who was in the perfumery business. He used to advertise his products—hair oil, scent and paan-masala—through a four-line rhyme. Every newspaper carried it:

Rub in your hair Kuntaleen,
On your hankie dab Delkhose;
With your paan chew Tambuleen,
And gratify Mister H Bose.

There was another business H Bose ran for sometime. He went
into collaboration with a French company and produced
gramophone records. We heard these records as children. They
used to rotate anti-clockwise, and the sound-box and needle
moved from the inside to the outside of the record.

Shona Thakuma had fourteen children. She lived until the
age of eighty. Even at that age, her hair was absolutely black,
and all her teeth were intact. Her complexion, too, remained as
fair as ever. She had four daughters. The oldest among them,
called Malati, became a well-known singer. Her eldest son,
Hiten, was a gifted painter, a connoisseur of classical music,
knew Persian and collected rare books. Like his mother, he was
fair and very good looking.

Nitin Bose (whom I called Putul Kaka) was one of his
brothers. He eventually became a well-known cameraman and
film director. I remember him taking a small movie camera to
Assam and returning with pictures of elephants being captured.
Afterwards, he sold the film to an English company.

Nitin was followed by Mukul. There was something wrong
with one of his legs, and he walked with a limp. His formal
education did not go very far, but he had an amazing
understanding of machinery. The famous botanist, Jagadish
Bose, trusted no one but Mukul Bose in the entire city of
Calcutta to handle and repair the delicate instruments he used
for his research. In later life, Mukul Bose also joined the film
industry and became a successful sound recordist.

The four brothers after Mukul—Kartik, Ganesh, Bapi and
Babu—all played cricket. When I was small, Kartik was

beginning to make a name for himself. Most people seemed to agree that no Bengali had ever played as well as Kartik Bose. Anyone visiting their house in Amherst Street in the evening would have seen both Kartik and Ganesh standing before a mirror and practising strokes. Behind their house was a concrete pitch. They had special bats for practising. The sides of these bats were scraped off, leaving only the middle portion to play with. I knew of no other house as full of fun and laughter as that of the Boses in Amherst Street.

Growing up in a Brahmo household, there was only one thing that I minded. It was the lack of fanfare in the Brahmo annual festival, which was called Maghotsav. Devoid of the noise and excitement that were so much part of a Hindu puja, Maghotsav simply consisted of devotional songs and long sermons that lasted for nearly two hours. We also had memorial services in our house every time there was a death in the family. Chairs and tables from our drawing room were removed, and a carpet spread on the marble floor. There were the inevitable songs and prayers. My mother was a good singer, so she sang each time. Sometimes, even those who could not sing all that well—such as Dhon Dadu and Kakamoni—also took part. After sitting with my head bowed and staring down at the same carpet year after year, I came to know the designs and patterns on it by heart.

The other thing I could never forget were the Sanskrit prayers and hymns that were chanted, and their meaning in Bengali intoned by the acharyas (ministers) in a particular way. Each word was elongated for some reason. For instance, the first three lines of *Asato ma sadgamaya* were explained thus:

Le-e-ad us from
Untru-u-th into Tru-u-th
Le-e-ad us from Da-a-rkness into Li-i-ght
Le-e-ad us from D-e-ath into E-e-ternal Li-i-fe!

Each acharya intoned these words in exactly the same way. Why no one ever thought of uttering them normally, I could never figure out.

There are two Brahmo temples in Calcutta, one in Cornwallis Street and the other in Bhowanipur. We continued to go to the former to celebrate Maghotsav even after moving to Bhowanipur. Although the festival took place in January, we had to get up at half past four in the morning to have a bath before going to the temple. The first hour was spent in Brahma keertan (praise for the Lord). It was followed by more songs and prayers. We had to sit on straight-backed wooden benches so there was never any question of comfort.

Only on three days of the festival did we have any fun. On the first day, we could have *khichuri* after the prayers; on the second day, there was a picnic; and the third day was set aside for children. There were no prayers that day, and we were free to enjoy ourselves. Even so, this Brahmo festival lacked the pomp and gaiety of Durga or Kali puja. We did take part in the celebrations for Kali puja (Diwali) although the pleasure we got from our simple sparklers and crackers and bangers have now been drowned totally in the ear-splitting, heart-stopping racket that the festival has inevitably come to mean. But the fact remains that no Brahmo festival could ever hold the whole city together in a joint merrymaking. Perhaps that was the reason why we were keen to celebrate Christmas and make it a part of our lives.

Whiteway Laidlaw was the biggest shop in Calcutta in those days. It was like a modern departmental store. The office of the *Statesman* stood where the Metro cinema now stands in Chowringhee. Next to it, at the corner of Suren Banerjee Road, was Whiteway Laidlaw, a building with a clock on it. The entire first floor of this huge building turned into a toyland during the few days leading up to Christmas. Once my mother took me to see it.

At that time the British were still ruling our country. Whiteway was owned by them. The sales people, as well as most of the customers, were white. My eyes were dazzled by these glamorous people. We were supposed to go up to the first floor. But where was the staircase? There were no stairs immediately visible, but there was a lift. That was the first time I saw a lift. It is likely that the lift installed by Whiteway Laidlaw was the first one in Calcutta.

An iron cage which had been painted golden carried us up to the toyland. When I stepped into the store I felt as if I had arrived in a land of dreams. A large part of the floor was taken up by hills, rivers, bridges, tunnels, stations, signals and a toy train that went on a mini railway track. In addition to these there were balloons, paper chains, streamers, artificial flowers and fruits and Chinese lanterns. A Christmas tree stood in all its glory, covered with colourful balls and silver stars. But what impressed me the most was a massive figure of Father Christmas: fat and rosy cheeks with a long white beard, a red coat and a red hat, and a big smile on his face.

The toys in the store were all foreign. I returned home with a box of crackers, which was the only thing we could afford to buy. One does not get to see crackers like those any more. The noise they made was as impressive as the tiny gifts that popped out from them.

Most of the large and attractive stores were in Chowringhee. But there was an Indian shop near Whiteway called Carr & Mahalanabis. It sold gramophones and sports equipment. We knew one of its Bengali owners. I called him Bula Kaka. His shop had a special chair that was actually a weighing machine. None of us could pass Bula Kaka's shop without going in, sitting in that chair and getting ourselves weighed. After my father died, it was Bula Kaka who gave me a gramophone. That was how I developed an interest in gramophones and records. I also had two toy gramophones. One of them was called Pigmyphone and the other was Kiddiphone. There were quite a few small records of Western music that went with them, each the size of a puri.

Bula Kaka did something else for me. He gave me a radio set on my birthday, soon after the radio station opened in Calcutta. It was quite different from modern radios, in that one had to use headphones to listen to it. This meant that it could be heard by only one person at a time. It was known as a crystal set.

Once, Bula Kaka took us to the Outram Restaurant. This rather posh restaurant floated on the water at Outram Ghat. It looked exactly like the deck of a ship. Outram Ghat has changed so radically over the years that it is very difficult to imagine what it looked like in the past. Fancy gas lights used to shine in the Eden Gardens opposite the ghat, and in the middle of it, an English band used to play in the evening.

It was in the Outram Restaurant that I had my first ice cream. I was teased about it for a long time afterwards, for as my teeth started aching after just the first spoonful, I happened to ask for the ice cream to be warmed up!

Bhowanipur

The business of U Ray & Sons folded up soon after they
stopped publishing the children's magazine, *Sandesh*. I was
too young to wonder about the reasons. All I can remember is
my mother telling me one day that we would have to leave the
house in Gorpar.

We moved to Bhowanipur to live with my mother's family,
away from Gorpar and north Calcutta. I was almost six at the
time. I was unaware of the change in my circumstances, or that
we had ceased to be wealthy and would have to live in a smaller
house. I do not think children are ever bothered by such things.
It is adults who decide who is to be pitied. It makes no difference
to children.

I was not sad, but taken aback by certain things I found in
my uncle's house in Bokulbagan, which was in Bhowanipur.
The first among these was the floor in the house. It was
embedded with pieces of china. I had never seen anything like
it before. I used to stare at the pieces and think, 'My God, how
many cups and saucers and plates were broken to make this
floor?' Most of the pieces were white, only a few had the
occasional flower, or a star or a wavy line. I could spend hours
just looking at these pieces of china on the floor.

The other thing I found here which was missing in Gorpar
was a balcony that overlooked the street. It was just outside my
bedroom. I could see all kinds of people from my balcony.
Hawkers went by in the afternoon, carting their colourful wares

and shouting, 'German stuff for two annas! Japanese for two annas!' Two or three times a week, a man with a box from a Mrs Wood used to be seen. My heart used to dance with joy if I heard my mother or any of my aunts call out to him: 'Come here, boxwalla!' It meant that tea that evening would be an interesting affair, for the man's box was always filled with delicious cakes, pastries and patties made by Mrs Wood.

Just as dusk began to gather, a man would turn up singing, '*Main laya hoon mazeda-a-r chanachu-u-r garam chanachur*!' We would wait eagerly to have this savoury hot snack. Only a few minutes later, someone in the house of the Chatterjees from across the road would start practising classical music in a raucous voice with a harmonium for accompaniment.

On hot summer afternoons, even after all doors and windows had been shut, the afternoon light used to seep in through the chinks in the shutters at a special hour, and display on the opposite wall inverted images from the street. I could see people walking, cycles, rickshaws and cars moving in different directions in that tightly shut room, as if by magic. I spent many an afternoon lying in my room, watching this free bioscope.

The front door of our house had a small hole. If the door was shut, and a piece of glazed glass was held before this hole, it was possible to see images from the street on this glass, each one upside down and in miniature form. This was nothing extraordinary. In fact, this is the basic principle of photography. Anyone can try it at home. But when I saw it for the first time as a child, I was absolutely fascinated.

My mother had four brothers. The youngest had died before I was born. Two of her other brothers worked as barristers in Patna and Lucknow. We moved in with her third brother, whom I called Shona Mama. He worked for a big Indian insurance company, which was owned by one of our relatives. Yet, Shona Mama never went to England and remained totally uninfluenced by the West throughout his life.

He had an astounding grasp of mathematics. Once, when I was in school, he happened to glance at a particularly complex problem on my maths question paper and said casually, 'The answer's eight, isn't it?' It seemed like magic to me.

Generally a quiet man, Shona Mama had a rather childlike side to him. He was nearly thirty, but he spent every Sunday playing games like carrom and ludo, and then bagatelle with great enthusiasm. He used to be joined by a lot of friends and relatives from his own age group. If they caught me in the room watching them, inevitably they said, 'Go on, Manik, away from the grown-ups!' At this, I had to leave the room, but I couldn't help thinking what my uncle and his friends were doing could hardly be described as adult behaviour.

I had to spend much of my time alone, particularly in the afternoon. But I never got bored. There were ten volumes of *The Book of Knowledge*. I never grew tired of leafing through these. Then, later, my mother bought me four volumes of *The Romance of Famous Lives*. These were biographies of famous foreigners, packed with illustrations and pictures.

There was something else to help me pass the time. It was an amazing contraption called a stereoscope. Many families

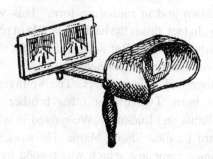

possessed one in those days but now this Victorian invention cannot be seen anywhere. It had a handle at the bottom. There was a frame that had a pair of flint glasses mounted on it. One had to hold the handle and peer through these. The picture stood in a holder fixed behind the frame. It was not a single picture, but two pictures placed side by side on a card. They looked identical, but that was not really the case. It was, in fact, the same scene, but shot with a camera with two lenses. The left lens captured what the left eye saw, and the right lens did the same for the right eye. Viewed through the glasses, the two pictures merged into one, and the scene acquired a three-dimensional effect. Different pictures for stereoscopes were available from many countries.

There was another gadget I often amused myself with, and that was a magic lantern. These, too, have now vanished. It looked like a box, and had a lens, a chimney and a handle. There were also two reels. One had to rotate the handle to wind the film from one reel to another. The film ran just behind the lens. A kerosene lamp burnt inside the box, expelling its smoke through the chimney. The light from the lamp threw moving images from the revolving film onto a wall. Who knows, perhaps my passion for films began with these magic lanterns?

Among Shona Mama's companions was a man called

Kalu, who lived in the same house in Bokulbagan. I looked upon him as another uncle and called him Kalu Mama, although he was no relation. He used to be Shona Mama's neighbour when they both lived in Dhaka. He had come to Calcutta to look for a job. Within six months of finding one, he bought a new Raleigh cycle for thirty rupees. He took such good care of it that, six months later, it still looked brand new.

Shona Mama was fond of having fun. After moving to his house, I began to get the chance to go to the circus, magic shows and carnivals. Once I went to watch a European magician called Shefallo at Empire Theatre (the modern Roxy). He performed trick after trick, talking incessantly. I learnt later that this non-stop chatter from a magician is called 'patter'. It was his patter that made the audience look more at his face than at his hands, which helped him pull off all his tricks. But Shefallo was followed by a female magician called Madame Palarmo, who performed in absolute silence. I never saw anything like that again.

Some time later, I happened to watch a Bengali magician at a wedding party, whose skills made Shefallo's performance on the stage pale into insignificance. If a magician is performing on a stage, he can use sophisticated equipments and appropriate lighting to hoodwink the audience. The man I saw at this wedding sat on a mattress under a shamiana, surrounded by other guests. Even so, he did an astounding number of tricks. Many years later, I used this magician as a character in a short story.

I saw him spread several matchsticks on the sheet that covered the mattress, and keep an empty matchbox with him. Then he opened the matchbox and called, 'Come on now, all of you, one by one!' Each matchstick rolled towards the box and slipped into it. Then he took a silver coin from a gentleman and a ring from another. He placed the coin at least four feet away from the ring. 'Go and bring the coin!' he said to the ring, which began rolling towards the coin like an obedient child. It stopped as it reached the coin, then both came back to the magician.

His third trick involved a pack of cards. He handed it to one of the guests, and borrowed a walking stick from someone else. Then he pointed the stick at the pack of cards and said, 'Come out then, ace of spades!' The ace of spades slipped out at once and sat fluttering at the end of the stick.

A few days later, I bumped into the magician near my house. He was in his early fifties, clad in a dhoti and a shirt, and looked no different from other ordinary men. Who could tell he had such extraordinary talent? I was very interested in magic myself and had already started to think of this man as my guru. 'I'd like to learn magic from you,' I said to him. 'Sure!' he replied, and taking out a pack of cards from his pocket, taught me a simple trick at once. But I never met him again. In my excitement at having run into him so unexpectedly, I had forgotten to take his address. Later, I bought quite a few books on magic and practised sleight of hand standing before a mirror. My interest in magic continued until I went to college.

The circus still comes to Calcutta, though they are now owned and run by South Indians. In our time, Europeans used to work in the Harmestone Circus. But what has disappeared altogether are carnivals. When I was a child, acres of empty land used to lie on both sides of Central Avenue. The first ten-storey highrise of Calcutta had not been built; nor had Victoria House—which now supplies electricity—come into existence. The carnival used to take place on one of these open fields, close to the circus.

It is difficult to explain to modern children what the carnival was like, and why we found it so enjoyable. Like the fairs we have today, it had giant wheels. But, unlike the ones we now get to see, those wheels were as high as a five-storey building. Their revolving lights could be seen from afar. Apart from these wheels, there were merry-go-rounds, dodgems, an alpine railway that went up and down, and much else. Spread out between these were stalls for gambling. The prizes displayed were so tempting that it was very difficult not to stop and have a go. Eventually, open gambling was banned by the government, which led to the extinction of the carnival in Calcutta. Gambling must have been a major source of income for them.

*

When we moved to Bhowanipur, talkies were yet to be made. The English cinemas had pianists to provide music throughout a film, instead of words. Only one theatre had something called a cinema organ. It was Madan, or the Palace of Varieties. It is now called Elite. The organ was known as the wurlitzer. It had a glorious sound. The Englishman who played it was called Byron Hopper. The daily papers carried lists of what Mr Hopper was going to play each day.

Among the films I saw at that time, I remember four in particular. They were *Ben Hur, The Count of Monte Cristo, The Thief of Baghdad* and *Uncle Tom's Cabin*. The Globe theatre showed not just films, but live songs and dances as well. There used to be an additional safety-curtain which hung in front of the regular curtain. It was always filled with advertisements. The safety-curtain was the first to rise, followed by the regular one, revealing an empty stage. A white screen used to come down once the songs and dances were over, and then the film would start. A piano stood by the screen. The pianist had to play suitable music throughout, in keeping with the mood of the film.

Something funny happened when we went to watch *Uncle Tom's Cabin*. The whole family had gone to see it together. In

one scene, the black slave, Uncle Tom, rolled down a flight of
stairs after being whipped by his cruel master, Simon Legree,
and died. We were all furious with Legree. Then, towards the
end of the film, Tom's ghost came back to haunt Legree. Legree
picked up his whip and lashed out at the ghost, but Tom
continued to move forward, laughing. At this point, Kalu
Mama, who had been watching the film with his jaw hanging
open, could not take it any more. He shot up from his seat and
began shouting, oblivious to the presence of the large audience,
'That bastard's *still* whipping him? He can *still* do it? Wait, you
devil, you'll soon get your just deserts!'

The first talkie was made in Hollywood in 1928. Calcutta
got its first talkie a year later. Some of the films that followed,
for a year afterwards, were partially silent. Those that had sound
throughout were advertised as '100% Talkie'. The first one I
saw was probably *Tarzan the Ape Man*. It was showing at
Globe, but we could not get tickets on the first day. The uncle
who had gone with me took one look at my disappointed face
and realized I should not be taken home without trying
elsewhere.

The Albion Theatre (now called Regal) was not far from
Globe. We found tickets there, but it was for a Bengali film
called *Kaal Parinay* (Cursed Marriage). It became obvious
pretty soon that it was not a film suitable for young children.
My uncle turned to me and asked, more than once, 'Want to go
home?' But I paid no attention. Having gone all that way, I was
not about to return home without watching the whole thing. But
the film was so bad that it put me off Bengali films for quite a
while.

The uncle who had taken me to it was a cousin of my
mother's. Like Kalu Mama, he had come from Dhaka to
Calcutta to look for a job, and stayed in Shona Mama's house.

Here I ought to mention another cousin of my mother's,

called Noni, for I never saw another man quite like him. Noni Mama was six foot tall, ramrod straight, and always wore a short dhoti, and a khaddar kurta with three-quarter sleeves. He used to walk very briskly in a military style, and speak loudly in his local East Bengal dialect. People in rural areas often speak loudly, possibly because they have to make themselves heard across open fields. Some people bring that habit to cities. Noni Mama was one of them. But, although he spoke loudly, there was something oddly feminine about the way he spoke. Also, he never got married. If he had, his wife would probably have found it difficult to match his expertise in housework. Noni Mama was an expert both in cookery and sewing. Later in life, he learnt leatherwork and even wrote a book on it. He wrote another book called *The Sweets of Bengal* but for some reason, it was never published.

My mother learnt leatherwork from Noni Mama and became an expert herself. She would sometimes spend whole afternoons working on pieces of leather, mixing spirit with the dyes she used. As a result, our room used to be filled with the smell of spirit. She eventually sold quite a few bags, wallets and spectacle cases, all beautifully made. After this, my mother learnt clay-modelling from the famous potter, Nitai Pal. Many of our relatives have still got the statues of Buddha and Pragya Paramita that she made.

In addition to all this, my mother was an extremely efficient housewife. Her handwriting, too, was beautiful, both in Bengali and English.

*

Shona Mama had an Erskine Sedan car, which is a make few will have heard of in this age of Fiats and Ambassadors. Sometimes we used to go for a drive in his car to the Maidan (the open space near Victoria Memorial, which still exists). Loads of Englishmen used to play golf there in the evening, so one could not walk in peace without having to watch out for flying golf balls. On one occasion, one of these balls nearly hit me. I was a bit preoccupied and did not see it coming. Luckily, our driver Sudheer Babu did, and quickly pulled me aside just in time to avoid serious damage. The ball flew past my ear and disappeared towards the railing of Victoria Memorial.

Sudheer Babu lived in the attic of our house. It was the time of Mahatma Gandhi's non-cooperation movement. Sudheer Babu brought a huge spindle one day, together with a bag of cotton, and began spinning, to make his own contribution to the movement. Gradually, almost like a contagious disease, this business of spinning thread spread through the city. Like every other family, ours got its own share of spindles. Even I was given one, and soon found myself spinning and producing thread like everyone else. But no one could beat Sudheer Babu. He actually had a short kurta made from the thread he had spun.

A big Swadeshi mela was held in Calcutta at that time, where we all went. There used to be a vast open field near Elgin Road, which has now been built upon, known as the Gymkhana

Grounds. That was where the mela was held. The most striking displays there were wax figures of famous Indian leaders. What made them special was that they had mechanical devices to move certain parts of their bodies. Different scenes had been created in separate cubicles. In one, Mahatma Gandhi sat writing on the floor in a prison cell, with an armed guard at the door. Gandhiji had a writing pad on his lap, and a pen in his hand. His hand moved across the pad from one side to the other, and his head followed the movement of his hand. In another cubicle, there was an enormous statue of Bharat Mata, with the body of Deshbandhu Chittaranjan Das in her arms. She looked at Deshbandhu, then closed her eyes and turned her head away mournfully. I do not know who made these waxworks— possibly someone in Bombay—but they were amazingly lifelike. These figures created a huge stir in Calcutta.

*

My maternal grandmother, Didima, lived with us in Bokulbagan. She was fair, slim and beautiful. She could also sing very well. Even now I can remember her singing a song from Mymensingh, *Charkar nachon deikhya ja lo tora* (Come and see the spinning wheel dance). It was probably in 1926 that all her children visited Calcutta along with their spouses and offsprings. This was a rather unusual event. Two uncles came from Patna and Lucknow, and an aunt from Kakina in East Bengal which was then a part of undivided India.

It was decided, when everyone had arrived, that a family photo would be taken with Didima. Not many houses had cameras in those days. The few that did, only had small box cameras which were not suitable for group photos, certainly not the kind fit to be framed and hung. So, on special occasions, people went to studios to have their photos taken. There were two very well-known studios in Calcutta, Bourne & Shepherd and Johnston & Hoffman. Both were nearly seventy years old at the time, and not doing very well. So we went to Edna Lorenz, which was a modern studio, and quite well known. It was situated in Chowringhee Mansions, at the corner of Chowringhee and Park Street. There were eighteen people in our group, including a small baby.

We had informed the studio previously and were expected, so all the necessary arrangements had been made. Six chairs had been placed in a row in a large hall. My grandmother took a chair in the middle. My mother and the other women sat on the other chairs. The men stood in rows behind them. Two young cousins sat on little stools before the ladies, and I stood between my mother and grandmother. Although the photo was going to be taken inside a room, no flash or artificial light was going to be used. Perhaps that was not the normal practice then. The only light available was what was coming in through a row of windows. The camera was very large, its lens covered by a cap. The cap would be removed for just a couple of seconds, and the photo would be taken in that time. No one was allowed to move during those two seconds.

The English photographer shouted, 'Ready!' and everyone became stiff, staring at the camera. There was another man standing next to the photographer, holding a toy in his hand. It was the figure of a clown, clutching a pair of cymbals. When its stomach was pressed, it played the cymbals noisily. This was necessary to make sure that the baby, who was seated on his mother's lap, looked straight at the camera when the photo was taken. Luckily, all went according to plan. The photographer's assistant got the clown to work, the baby looked in the right direction and the photographer did his job successfully.

Within five years of this group photo being taken, my grandmother, an uncle and a cousin died. Dhon Dadu used the

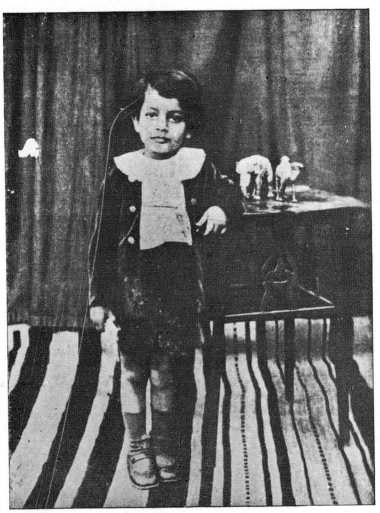

When Ray was two years old, some time before his father died

Right and bottom right: photographs
taken when Ray was four years old

With his grandmother and cousin Shorol

Some pages from Ray's autograph book.

Top: Leela Pishi's sketch.

Right and bottom: Nandalal Bose's drawings of a bear and a tiger, both done in 1925

Rabindranath Tagore's poem from Ray's autograph book.

Hazaribagh. 1925. Front row: Nini, Ruby and Lalita.
Behind them from the left: Kalyanda, Mejo Pishima, Binadi and Ray

Probably 1928, Lucknow. Front row from left: Ray, his mother with Bachchu on her lap, Montu, Mejo Mami with Bablu on lap.
Back row: Shona Mami, Mejo Mama and Chhoto Mashi

Chhoto Mashi Kanak Das (later Biswas), 1928

Shona Mama Proshantokumar Das, 1926

In Darjeeling with Avinash Meshomoshai and family
(Ray is fourth from the left)

Bula Kaka, 1932

One of eight photographs taken at the
same sitting in 1932

Chhoto Kaka   Subimal Ray

Ray with his mother. Ray took this photograph himself by pulling a thread tied to the shutter of the camera

Dhon Dadu Kuladaranjan Ray

Some of the boys from the club at Beltola Road. Taken in 1934 with Ray's box camera Fouth from the left in the middle row is Manu (Siddhartha Shankar Ray). To his right is Panu

Off to the Sunderbans

A dip in the sea

same photo to make enlargements of all three faces.

*

My mother's youngest sister—Chhoto Mashi to me—lived with us. She, too, was a gifted singer. But whenever she was asked to sing before an audience, she became nervous and her throat dried up. It was only her close family who could ever get to hear her sing freely.

However, one day, Bula Kaka arranged for her to record a song for HMV. They probably knew him well and respected him, as he was one of the owners of the famous gramophone shop, Carr & Mahalanabis.

Chhoto Mashi was required to go to the recording studio of HMV. I went with her in Bula Kaka's red model-T Ford. Tense and nervous, Chhoto Mashi had hardly eaten anything in the last couple of days. Bula Kaka kept up a constant flow of reassurance—there was nothing to it, really, everything would be all right. He himself never sang, but could play Tagore songs on the flute. He also played the organ.

The HMV company was then owned and run purely by Englishmen. Its manager and sound recordist were both English. In those days, there were no microphones. One had to sing facing a funnel-like horn; the song would then be printed on a revolving wax disc in the next room.

Chhoto Mashi had drunk endless glasses of water that morning. Still apprehensive, she went and stood before the horn. I watched her from the next room through a glass partition. A young recordist arrived and adjusted the horn for her. Then he took out a packet of cigarettes from his pocket, extracted one and threw it into the air. He caught it between his lips as it fell, lit it, and left the room. Bula Kaka told us afterwards that in the presence of a female singer, this recordist was often wont to show off. It is my belief that his cigarette-juggling antics, if anything, added to my aunt's anxieties.

Anyway, she finally sang when she was asked to, though I could tell she was still feeling self-conscious. The record was released some time later. Eventually, she recorded several songs and became an established singer. Her name was Kanak Das. After her marriage, she became Kanak Biswas.

*

One of my father's brothers, Subinay Ray, lived quite close to our house in Bokulbagan. He revived the *Sandesh* magazine, which had ceased to be published two years after my father's death in 1923. At the time, I was too young to read it. Now, after its revival, I came to know what it felt like to hold a freshly printed magazine and read its contents. Three different colours were used on the cover. It showed an elephant standing on two feet with a pot of the Bengali sweetmeat sandesh balanced on its trunk.

Among the contributors to the revived *Sandesh* was Rabindranath Tagore. His story called 'Shay' was serialized from the first issue. Leela Majumdar—the well-known writer—published her first story in *Sandesh*. The funny illustrations that accompanied her stories were her own. Another artist and illustrator of repute in Bengal, Shaila Chakravarty, also began his career by drawing for *Sandesh*.

There was another Bengali magazine for children at that time called *Ramdhonu*, which I liked very much. I remember how much I enjoyed meeting its editor, Manoranjan Bhattacharya, for I had read two of his stories—'Padmaraag' and 'Ghosh-Chowdhury's Clock'—and found them immensely enjoyable. They were detective stories, and the detective was a Japanese called Hukakashi.

It was while living in Bokulbagan that I learnt to swim at the Bhowanipur Swimming Club. This was at a time when Prafulla Ghosh, the famous swimmer, had created a world record by staying in the water for seventy-six hours, after having rubbed his body with lard. At about the same time, the world champion American swimmer, Johnny Weissmuller, had played the part of Tarzan and startled everyone. I found a photograph of Weissmuller at my club, with his autograph on it. This made me look upon the club with new respect. I spent the first few years simply kicking my feet in the water, holding on to bamboo poles for support. But eventually, I did learn to swim properly and found myself swimming across the pond and back.

During those days, many people used to give great importance to making children exercise regularly to keep fit. I do not know how passionately people believe in it these days. Many men, in my time, used to do press-ups. Those with a greater awareness of health and fitness used dumb-bells and chest expanders. I was not all that keen on doing exercises, but another great-uncle, Pramadaranjan Ray, made sure that I wasn't spared. Pramadaranjan himself had spent his life as a geological surveyor, going through impenetrable jungles and visiting other remote corners of the country. He could not stand even the hint of femininity in a man. In fact, he had reservations against the long, wavy hair Tagore sported. I was made to join his sons to keep fit.

Talking of doing exercises, I must mention how I learnt ju-jitsu, although that happened in 1934, by which time I had left Bokulbagan and moved to Beltola Road.

It was in Shantiniketan that I first saw ju-jitsu being practised. I was about ten years old then. My mother and I had gone to attend Poush Mela, a festival held annually in Shantiniketan every December. I had bought a new autograph book, with a view to having its first page signed by Tagore.

I went to Uttarayan one morning. Tagore took my autograph book, but said, 'Leave it with me. You can collect it tomorrow.'

We returned the next day. He was sitting at his desk, which was piled high with letters, various pieces of paper, books and notebooks. He began looking for my little purple autograph book as soon as he saw me. It took him nearly three minutes to find it. Then he handed it to me, looked at my mother and said, 'He will understand the meaning of these words only when he's older.' What he had written was a short poem, which is known to most people today:

It took me many days, it took me many miles;
I spent a great fortune, I travelled far and wide,
To look at all the mountains,
And all the oceans, too.
Yet, I did not see, two steps away from home,
Lying on a single stalk of rice:
A single drop of dew.

It was during this visit that I saw ju-jitsu and judo at Shantiniketan. Buddhist lamas in ancient China had developed this form of unarmed combat to protect themselves against robbers and bandits. It travelled from China to Japan, and from Japan to the rest of the world. Tagore saw people practising judo in Japan, and decided that his students in Shantiniketan should be taught this art. The Japanese expert, Takagaki, soon arrived in Shantiniketan and began judo lessons. For some unknown reason, these classes ran only for about four years, after which Takagaki moved to Calcutta. He rented the ground floor from one of my uncles, Dr Ajitmohan Bose, in Ballygunj and began giving lessons.

Purely out of the blue, one day my Chhoto Kaka, Subimal, turned up at our house and said, 'Why don't we learn judo?'

Subimal was the same uncle who chewed every mouthful thirty-two times. Anyone who had seen him would know how difficult it was to connect him with anything sporty like wrestling or judo, or any other form of vigorous exercise. Thin and absent-minded, he had worked as a schoolteacher after doing his MA. He was a simple peace-loving man. Why did he want to learn judo? Where was the need for him to learn it? But he had clearly made up his mind. He left in a tram to find Swinhoe Street in Ballygunj, taking me with him.

It is impossible to imagine the difference between Ballygunj as it stands today, and the Ballygunj of 1934, unless one has seen both. A little way down Rashbehari Avenue, past the Mahanirvan monastery, the road was lined with mango, jamun and jackfruit trees, and endless leafy bushes. There were virtually no houses to be seen. The area looked more like a village than a part of a large city.

We had to get off at the corner of Gariahat, and cross a field dotted with bamboo groves, palms and coconut trees to reach Takagaki in Swinhoe Street. My uncle had probably telephoned to warn him of our arrival. It took us very little time to find the right house, meet the judo expert, who was clad in a purple kimono, and finalize all arrangements. The man was about forty, had jet black crew-cut hair and dark eyebrows, and a moustache to match. I was expecting him to start laughing on being told that Chhoto Kaka wanted to learn judo. On the contrary, he behaved as if he thought my uncle would make an ideal student. A tailor arrived soon to measure us for our special judo garments: a jacket made of thick cotton (a bit like khaddar), a belt and short pyjamas. Across the front of the jacket, stitched in large black letters was the word 'JUDO'.

We began lessons when our costumes were ready. A

ten-inch thick mattress was spread on the floor. Forty-five years later, I can recall only two intricate holds: sheoi-nage and nippon-shio. The first lessons simply taught us how to throw someone on the floor, and how to fall. One of the basic things that judo teaches is how to fall without causing oneself a lot of damage. Takagaki told us to relax the body as far as possible while falling. This reduced pain upon impact with the floor and minimized the chances of a fracture. Throwing someone else involved raising them over one's head before hurling them down. If one used the special techniques of judo, a young boy of thirteen could overpower a large and hefty adult with surprising ease.

Two other gentlemen used to join us on the days we visited Takagaki. One of them was a Bengali and a trainee, like ourselves. The other was an Englishman, an army man called Captain Hughes, who lived in Fort William. He was a light heavyweight boxing champion in Calcutta. A good-looking man with clear, sharp features, he had short, wavy golden hair. He already knew judo. He came to Takagaki simply to practise what he had learnt, for there was no one else in Calcutta to rival him. Their fights were always extraordinary affairs. We used to watch them, spellbound. Hold after hold, throw after throw, it went on, until one of them found himself in an awkward

position and admitted defeat by thumping the mattress twice.
The other then loosened his hold and let him go.

At the end of each session Takagaki offered us Ovaltine.
It was usually dark by the time we left, crossed the same field
with all those trees, and caught a tram to go back home.

*

As a result of moving from north to south Calcutta we lost touch
with many relatives on my father's side. The two people who
continued to visit us frequently were Chhoto Kaka (the judo
enthusiast), and Dhon Dadu. Dadu was translating Conan
Doyle into Bengali at the time. He used to dress like a pukka
sahib: a suit made by the well-known tailor, Barkat Ali, with a
tie if he went out in the evening. He came to our house at least
three times a week.

It was Dadu who told me all the stories from the
Mahabharat. We used to read a chapter a day. I made him tell
me one particular story at least four times. It was the story of
Jayadrath being killed in battle by Arjun. I thought it was the
most thrilling story of all. Absolutely fascinated, I heard how,
one day, Arjun vowed to kill Jayadrath before sunset and
eventually did, with a bit of help from Krishna. But that was not
all. The chopped head of Jayadrath could not be allowed to
touch the ground, for Jayadrath's father's curse would then
work on Arjun and Arjun's own head would be blown off. In a
rather clever move, Arjun struck the head with six more arrows
before it could reach the ground, and made it fly a great distance
to land in the lap of Jayadrath's father. Startled, his father stood
up, the chopped head fell on the ground, and his father's head
was immediately blown to pieces.

Dadu told me stories from the Mahabharat, and Chhoto
Kaka told me ghost stories. It is not easy to describe briefly what

kind of person my uncle was, for I doubt very much if any other
man could ever be found who was quite like him.

He taught at the City School. His short dhoti, his kurta with
loose sleeves, the chadar on his shoulder, the umbrella in his
hand, and the brown canvas shoes on his feet, all proclaimed
his profession. He never got married. It was perhaps because
he was alone in the world that he could find the time to either
walk or take a bus to visit all our relatives. He was the only one
in our huge, scattered family who was in touch with everyone
else.

I do not know if people who are eccentric always have
peculiar dreams, but that seemed to be the case with Chhoto
Kaka. Once he dreamt that he'd gone to a keertan. The singers
were singing only one line over and over, 'In truth do
aubergines burn!' He even sang the line for us. Then, one night,
he dreamt that a vast number of monkeys had taken out a
procession, chanting, 'Strength and power! More in our
opium—strength and power!'

Chhoto Kaka had given nicknames to many of our
relatives, and referred to them only by those names. Soon, we
all became familiar with them. Dhon Dadu was 'Dedux'. An
uncle called Arun was 'Voroid'; and Dhon Dadu's daughter,
Tutu Pishi, was 'Wang', and his son, Panku Kaku, was 'Gogril';
two female cousins were referred to as 'Big Kusumpua' and
'Small Kusumpua'; my mother was 'Bojro Bouthan' and I was
'Nulmuli'. Nobody knew quite why these names had come into
being. Once I asked him why Uncle Arun was called 'Voroid'.
Chhoto Kaka replied gravely, 'Because he gets up at the crack
of dawn.' (The Bengali word for dawn is *bhor*.)

Chhoto Kaka was not overtly religious, but had a natural
curiosity about sadhus and sanyasis. He read about their lives,
and truly respected many of them. Tibbati Baba, Trailanga
Swami, Vijaykrishna Goswami, Santdas Babaji and Ramdas

Kathiababa were among them. If any of them happened to be in town, Chhoto Kaka went and visited them. I heard a lot about these men from him.

Living by himself, doing his own thing, happy with what little he possessed in life, sometimes Chhoto Kaka himself appeared to be a sort of sadhu. Besides, he had a few habits which set him apart from other men. I have already talked about how he chewed every mouthful thirty-two times. During his morning ablutions, he often spent a long time drawing water through his nose and bringing it out through his mouth. This exercise was called naki-mudra. There was also something called kaki-mudra, but I cannot now recall what it entailed. In the evening, he lay inert on his bed doing another Yoga exercise called shavasan, before grabbing his umbrella and going out.

In spite of the time he spent on his varied activities, Chhoto Kaka also maintained a diary. I can say with some confidence that no one has ever made entries in a diary the way he did. He recorded such details as the headlines in the day's papers, his activities every hour, including what he read, what he ate, where he went, and who he saw. If he travelled by rail anywhere, he would record the engine type. It was from Chhoto Kaka that I learnt engines could be of various types. XP, HPS, SB, HB—were the various type names. In those days, steam engines used to have these types written on them.

Chhoto Kaka always tried to reach the station well before the train departed, for he knew he would have to dash out again to look at the letters on the engine as soon as he had placed his baggage on his seat. If, for some reason, he could not do this before the train started, he would get off at the first junction it stopped at and quickly note down the type before rushing back to his seat.

The ink he used to write in his diary was of four different colours—red, blue, green and black. Sometimes he used all four colours to write just one sentence. There was a reason why he switched from one colour to another, but I could never grasp it fully. All I could fathom was that descriptions of nature were to be written in green, and all nouns had to be in red. For instance, if he had to write something like 'It rained heavily today. Couldn't go to Manik's house', he would write the first sentence in green. The first three words of the next sentence would be in blue or black, but the last two would be in red. Before he started writing in his diary with grave concentration, Chhoto Kaka would place a small, low table on his bed and spread out all his pens and various bottles of ink, almost as if he was opening shop. It was an amazing sight.

There was something else that made his diaries special. I must explain it in some detail.

Chhoto Kaka was not greedy, but he enjoyed his food and, in fact, was something of a gourmet. He paid particular attention to the tea he drank each day at the various households he visited. He always found an appropriate description for the tea he tasted. This was recorded in his diary, but not in any ordinary way. Each type of tea would be given a label which would then be explained within brackets.

Here are a few examples, taken from entries made over a month. I hope this will make things clear:

1. Tea fit for Narasimha (brimming with valour, roar-inducing, powerful tea).
2. Tea fit for a Vaishnav (innocuous, sweet, soft, non-violent tea).
3. Tea worthy of Vivekananda (good-deed-encouraging, eloquence-enhancing, deeply philosophical, enjoyable tea).
4. A Brahmin's tea (wisdom-creating, gravity-forming, not-too-strong, hearty tea).

5. Tea for Dhanwantari, the physician of the gods (all-curing, life-prolonging, mineral-enriched tea).
6. A watchman's tea (stimulating, sleep-destroying tea).
7. Tea for get-togethers (chatty, relaxing tea).
8. A clerk's tea (book-keeping-encouraging, light brown, tasty tea).
9. Tea fit for a constable (officious, self-important, supercilious tea).
10. Tea for the masses (average, make-do tea).
11. Tea fit for Narad, the ancient sage who played the veena (musically-uplifting, religious-fervour-arousing tea).
12. Tea worthy of Hanuman (trust-arousing, innovative, vigorous, power-for-leaping-oceans tea).

Holidays

Within a couple of years after moving to Bhowanipur from Gorpar, my mother took a job in a school for widows called Vidyasagar Vanibhavan. She had to take a bus every day and travel all the way back to north Calcutta, to a place not far from Gorpar. During this time, she also used to look after my studies. I began to go to a school from the age of nine. When my mother's school closed during the summer and before Durga Puja, the two of us went on short holidays.

However, going on holidays was something we did even before we left Gorpar. I have a few memories of a visit to Lucknow, where we stayed first with my mother's cousin, Atulprasad Sen, and then with his sister, whom I called Chhutki Mashi. There was always music in Atul Mama's house, for he was a lyricist and composer. Often, he would get my mother to learn his songs, then write the words down for her in her black notebook. Ravi Shankar's guru, Alauddin Khan, used to stay in Atul Mama's house at that time. I heard him play the piano occasionally. One day, the well-known singer of those times, Sri Krishan Ratanjankar, visited us and sang his famous song, *Bhavani dayani*, set in Bhairavi. Atul Mama wrote a new song, *Shuno, shey dakey aamarey* (Listen, he's calling out to me), based on *Bhavani dayani*.

One day, my mother and Atul Mama took me to a lecture. Not only was it a lecture on classical music, but it was being delivered in English. I soon grew bored and began to nod off.

But each time that happened, I tried to rouse myself, partly because I did not wish to appear rude, and partly because my mother kept scolding me. I had no idea that the speaker was none other than Vishnu Narayan Bhatkhande. Few men in India could match his profound knowledge of music.

I could not enjoy myself much at Chhutki Mashi's place, for her husband, Srirangam Desikachar Seshadri Ayangar, was a Tamilian, and their three children could speak no Bengali. I had to remain silent most of the time, and listen to them speak fluent English. Only in the evenings could I join them in a game called Happy Families.

On that occasion, I remember, we were accompanied by my Chhoto Mashi (Kanak Das, the nervous singer I have mentioned before). Either on our way to or from Lucknow, my mother and Chhoto Mashi got into the inter-class compartment reserved for ladies. There was no room there for me, so I was pushed into the next carriage, which was a second-class compartment. I got into it, to find it packed with English men and women. This filled me with apprehension, but what could I do? The train started almost immediately, so there was no way I could get out and find another coach. Resigned to my fate, I sat quietly on the floor all night. God knows if any of those people wanted to offer me a seat. It would have made no difference, really, for if any of them had spoken to me, I could not have understood their accent. It is my belief that none of them was even aware of my presence.

I went back to Lucknow several times afterwards. One of my mother's brothers worked there as a barrister. His two sons—Montu and Bachchu—were younger than me, but they became my playmates. The city itself intrigued me a great deal. The Bara and Chhota Imambara, Chhattar Manzil, the Dilkhusha Gardens—all built by the nawabs—used to remind me of the Arabian Nights. What amazed me the most was the maze called Bhulbhulaiya inside the Bara Imambara. It was impossible to come out of unless one had a guide to show the way. I once heard from a guide the story of how an English soldier had walked into it without one, utterly confident that he could come out by himself. But he lost his way and remained in the maze for days, slowly starving to death.

Then there was the Residency. There were large holes in its broken walls, where the sepoys had bombarded it with their cannons. There was a marble plaque in a room, proclaiming the day and the time Sir Henry Lawrence had died. I could almost see it all happen. It was like living through a few pages of history. Much later in life, I mentioned Lucknow in my writing and showed it in a film. My childhood memories of the city made this task much easier than it might have been.

After our first visit to Lucknow, my mother took me to Shantiniketan. We spent three months there. I used to play with Rathindranath's (Rabindranath Tagore's son) adopted daughter, Pupey. She and I were more or less of the same age. Pupey used to come to our house every morning and play with me for an hour. At the time, Shantiniketan abounded with huge open spaces. To the south of the ashram was an endless expanse of khoaai, a series of shallow gorges cut into the earth by streams and rivulets, exposing the red earth. Whenever there was a full moon, my mother and I went out to the khoaai, and she sang, clearly and freely.

She had bought me a small notebook. Sometimes I went to the School of Fine Arts, Kala Bhavan, notebook in hand, to speak to the famous artist, Nandalal Bose. He drew me pictures of four animals. A cow and a leopard were drawn with a pencil; and with water colours, he drew a bear and a tiger. He finished drawing the tiger by putting a dark patch on the tip of its tail. 'What's that patch for?' I asked. 'This tiger,' Nandalal Bose explained, 'is very greedy. He walked into someone's kitchen to steal a piece of meat. That's when his tail got caught in a hot stove, and the tip was burnt!'

*

I was seven when I first went to Darjeeling. Three of my aunts lived there, and we were to take turns to stay with them all. I remember waking on the train on our way there and being greeted by the Himalayas. I was rendered absolutely speechless. Maya Mashima—with whom we were going to stay first of all—sent a car to Siliguri to meet us. We got into the car and began going up a road that bent and curved round a hill. As we rose higher, it became more cloudy, misty and hazy; but instead of reducing his speed, the driver drove faster and faster. Apparently, he knew the way like the back of his hand and so did not think there was any cause for concern.

Maya Mashima's husband (in whose house in Calcutta I learnt ju-jitsu) was a well-known doctor in Darjeeling. Their son, Dilip, was older than me by about five years. He could speak Nepali as fluently as the locals, and was often seen sitting by his gate with other Nepalis, playing cards. He also rode very well, galloping off as if he was Genghis Khan. He went on to work as a jockey for some years at the Lebong race course in Darjeeling. He was possibly the only Bengali jockey in the history of Darjeeling.

I enjoyed playing carrom with Dilipda. He also had loads of comic books. I have always enjoyed reading comics. If I happened to fall ill, my mother would go to New Market in Calcutta and buy me two new comics for four annas. What I enjoyed reading most were *Comic Cuts* and *Film Fun*.

From Maya Mashima's house, we went to stay with another aunt called Monu Mashi. Her husband, Avinash, owned the big insurance company where Shona Mama (my uncle in

Bokulbagan) worked. Their house was called Elgin Villa. They
had levelled the top of the hill in front of their house and built
a tennis court there. Avinash Meshomoshai (as I called him)
played tennis there with his two sons.

I must speak at some length about this particular uncle, for
many of my childhood memories are closely linked with events
at his massive house in Alipore's New Road in Calcutta.

Avinash Meshomoshai began his career as a clerk, but rose
to become the owner of the Empire of India Life Insurance
Company. When I saw him, he was no different from an English
gentleman in his dress and demeanour. It was impossible to
guess his humble beginnings. He had many children. One of his
sons, Amiyo, was Shona Mama's friend. I saw them flying kites
with silk thread from the roof of our house in Calcutta, although
they were certainly not of the right age to fly kites. I was.

A wedding in the house in New Road was always a grand
affair. Not only was the food always delicious, but there were
also arrangements to entertain the guests. When one of his
daughters got married, Avinash Meshomoshai got the famous
comedian, Professor Chittaranjan Goswami, to give a
performance. This kind of thing has now disappeared almost
totally. Very few now seem to have the ability to perform a solo
act that might keep the audience thoroughly entertained for an
hour or so. Chittaranjan Goswami was an expert at this. Even
today, I remember a few lines from one of his comic songs. It
had reminded me of a play my father had written called
Lakkhaner Shaktishel based on an event described in the
Ramayan. Professor Goswami's song went like this:

Ravan came to battle wearing a pair of boots
(and) Hanuman kicked him, slapped and poked him,
Crying, 'Oh you monstrous brute!'
(Glory be to Ram, oh glory be to Ram!)

These were the first few lines of the song. It ended with:

> With a whoosh the arrow pierced Ravan's chest,
> 'Oh God!' he cried, 'Ram's got me, the pest!'
> (Glory be to Ram!)
>
> Raising twenty arms, screaming through ten mouths,
> Such a mighty racket!
> In less than no time, did Ravan kick the bucket.
> (Glory be to Ram, oh glory be to Ram!)

When Professor Goswami finished singing this song—as only he could—we were all helpless with laughter. Then he stopped singing and coolly began eating rasgullas, stopping only after he'd eaten nineteen of them!

The same uncle in Alipore had an Italian car, a Lancia. On its bonnet was fixed a dragonfly made of glass. When the car moved, a pink light flickered through the dragonfly.

When we went to Darjeeling, my mother had not yet started working in Calcutta. But, during our stay in Darjeeling, she took the job of a teacher in Maharani Girls' School. I, too, joined the same school. It was a strange place. There were no separate classrooms. All classes took place in a large hall. I could see my mother teaching maths from where I sat in my corner, reading my own books. I cannot remember how long I spent in that school. God knows if I was really given lessons of some kind, or whether I was simply made to sit quietly until my mother was ready to go home.

I had been having a good time at Darjeeling ever since we arrived but one thing made me feel quite sad. It had been misty and hazy every day and I had not yet seen Kanchenjunga. My grandfather's painting of Kanchenjunga hung on a wall in our house in Calcutta. I was dying to see the real thing, to find out how it compared with the painting. At last, one day, while we were staying at Elgin Villa, my mother woke me very early in the morning. I ran and stood at the window.

In the painting, my grandfather had caught the evening sun falling on the snow, to the left of Kanchenjunga. Now, I could see the sun's first rays falling on its right.

I gaped open-mouthed, and watched the faint pink glow turn to golden, and from golden to a shimmering silver. Later in life, I got the chance to watch many beautiful sights both in my own country and abroad; but I do not think anything can match the beauty of Kanchenjunga during sunrise and sunset.

*

When it came to holidays, I enjoyed myself the most at the house of one of my father's sisters. I called her Mejo Pishima. She lived in Bihar with her husband, who worked as a deputy district officer. His job was a transferable one, so he travelled from Hazaribagh to Darbhanga, and then to Muzaffarpur and Ara. He was posted in Hazaribagh when I paid my first visit to their house. They had two daughters, Nini and Ruby. Two of their cousins called Kalyan and Lotu also lived with them. They had lost both parents, and were brought up by my aunt and uncle. All four of them were older than me, but they were my greatest friends.

I visited them several times in Hazaribagh. What I remember from my first visit is my uncle's green Overlander. If anyone saw it today, they would undoubtedly laugh at this shabby jalopy. But I had heard from my uncle, often enough, what a sturdy and reliable vehicle it was.

Once we drove to Rajrappa in the Overlander. It was about fifty miles from Hazaribagh; one had to cross a river called the Vehra, and thereafter walk for about a mile to reach the place.

It was a strange and wonderful spot. There was a waterfall, the river Damodar with its sandy banks, a forest in the distance, and the temple of Chhinnamasta (an incarnation of Kali which shows the goddess with her head chopped off). The temple gave me the creeps.

On our way back, the car broke down near the Brahmanberia Hills. I had heard that wild animals—including bears and tigers—frequented that area. It was dark by the time the car got going again, but I did not get to see a single animal.

Sometimes we went for long walks, returning just before dinner. It was great fun to sit by the dim light from lanterns and kerosene lamps and chat or play games. We often played cards. Two of the most popular games were called Aaina Mohur (Guinea Mirror) and Golam Chor (Jack the Thief). The latter is a game which is still played and everyone knows it. But I have never seen anyone playing Aaina Mohur. I do not even remember its rules now.

Among other enjoyable games was the 'whispering game'. To play it, five players had to sit in a circle. The first player was required to whisper something into the ear of the player on his left. One was allowed to speak only once. Then the second player would repeat what he had heard, whispering once more

to the third player. When the words finally came back to the first player, they bore very little resemblance to what was spoken originally. The greatest fun was to see how they had changed. On one occasion, I remember saying, 'Twinkle twinkle little star'. When it came back to me, it had become, 'Jiggle juggle pickle jar'. This game gets more interesting if ten or twelve players can join in.

When my aunt and uncle moved to Darbhanga and Ara, I visited them there. These two places were not as interesting as Hazaribagh, but that did not stop us from having loads of fun. Nini and Ruby were joined by another cousin called Dolly, so I had one more playmate.

The house in Darbhanga was a bungalow with a huge compound. There were several big trees, including mango, on one side of the compound. To the left of the house, in an open space, stood another huge mango tree from which hung a swing.

When I visited this house, the monsoon had started. A heavy shower often created little nullahs in the barren ground just below the swing. These carried the water with great force into the drains outside the house. We used to make paper boats and float them on the water. The little nullahs carried them straight into the drains that were like surging oceans.

At times, we imagined these boats to be the ships of the Vikings. A thousand years ago, there were pirates in Norway, who were called Vikings. It was our belief that if anyone died at sea, the Vikings cremated the dead in the ship. So we made tiny paper pirates and placed them in our boats. Then someone would strike a match to it and set the boat afloat. We called this the Viking's Funeral. Sadly, it was not just the Viking who got cremated, but the boat as well.

I was nine when I went to Ara. My aunt and her family lived there in a big, sprawling red brick house. On the ground floor, there were several rooms around a courtyard, some of which were not in use. There were more rooms upstairs. One of these was my uncle's study. There was a big garden, too, to match the size of the house.

Nini and Ruby's cousin, Kalyanda, was older than me by six years. He was, at that time, my greatest friend. He was an enthusiastic stamp-collector then. Inspired by him, I started doing the same, and bought packets of hinges, a pair of tweezers and a magnifying glass. This last object was necessary to see if there was an error anywhere on a stamp, for I had heard that an error always added to its value. So I began to reach for my magnifying glass the minute I found a stamp, be it an Indian or a foreign one. Was there an error in this one? No; nor in that one or in any of the others. To tell the truth, I could never find a stamp with an error. Perhaps that was why I lost interest after a while and gave up philately.

Kalyanda had another role to play, which ought to be described in some detail.

I have already mentioned my fascination for Christmas. At the time, I had an implicit belief in the existence of Father Christmas. Yes, of course there was an old man with a long white beard who arrived the night before Christmas and filled the stockings of small children with little gifts. There was really no reason to leave Christmas out of all the fun I had at Mejo Pishima's house. So what if it was not December? Who says you can't have Christmas in June?

So, one night during my stay in Ara, Kalyanda became Father Christmas. I found a pair of stockings and hung them from the railing by my bed. Then I went to bed, shut my eyes and pretended to be asleep. Kalyanda used cotton wool to make a beard and a moustache and stuck it on his face with glue. Then he found a sack, which was supposed to be full of gifts. It had to make a noise as he moved, to let me know that Father Christmas was really and truly coming into my room. Kalyanda filled the sack with empty tins and cans, and slung it over his shoulder.

Half an hour later, I heard the rattle of tins. Then, through half-closed eyes, I saw in the shadowy darkness, Kalyanda, dressed as Santa Claus, enter my room and stop by my bed. A second later, faint clinking noises told me something was being pushed into my stockings. I knew the whole thing was make-belief; yet I felt positively thrilled.

Dhon Dadu joined us on that occasion before we left Ara. He often went out on walks in the evening, accompanied by all the children. The Ara railway station was about a mile and a half from our house. We went there sometimes to stand on the platform and watch the Imperial Mail whoosh past, and hear its ear-splitting whistle. This train looked most impressive, with golden emblems painted on its pale yellow carriages. No other train at that time had such a glamorous appearance, or such terrible speed.

One evening, as we were all walking to the station (Dadu dressed like an Englishman, complete with a sola topee and a

walking stick), when a bull came charging out of nowhere. Shaking its horns and staring out of bloodshot eyes, it came running straight at us. I had never seen such a ferocious animal. 'Leave the road, get into the fields!' Dadu commanded.

Getting into the fields was not easy. Prickly pear lined the way, but neither Dadu nor we had the time to worry about it. We crashed through the cactus and went down a slope to stand in a field, quite oblivious to our cuts and bruises. From this distance, through the prickly pear and other bushes, we could see what Dadu was doing. He was standing still, his legs apart, holding his stick high above his head and rotating it like the propeller of an aeroplane. The angry bull, completely taken aback by the strange antics of this even stranger-looking human, had stopped short a few yards away from him, and was staring with frank curiosity.

The propeller continued to spin, but the bull could not take it for more than a minute, and beat a retreat. We crawled back to the road, this time moving more cautiously to avoid further injury.

*

Later during our visit, several other people from my family joined us in Ara. They were four of the eight children of my grandfather's brother, Pramadaranjan Ray. I have mentioned him before. He was the great-uncle who worked for the government's geological department, and had gone to difficult and remote corners of India and Burma. I came to know him only after he retired and moved close to our house in Bhowanipur. He was a very strong man, and had an implicit faith in physical exercise. If he saw any of us slouch, he would jab our backs sharply. His guffaw could be heard from one end of the road to the other, and his whistle was loud enough and sharp enough to startle the whole neighbourhood.

All his children were very good at studies. He had three daughters. The second of these, Leela Pishi (Leela Majumdar, who is now one of the editors of *Sandesh*), was known to me at the time as an illustrator. One of her brothers—also called Kalyan—was very quiet, known only for his habit of rising at four o'clock in the morning and having twenty-two rotis for dinner. Among his other brothers were Prabhat, Ami, Saroj and Jotu.

Ami had a fantastic collection of stamps; Saroj, at the time, was the tallest man in the family; and Jotu, who was conscious of his good looks, could not resist looking at himself in a mirror every now and then.

Prabhat was a brilliant mathematician. I grew very close to him because he came to our house frequently. Like Chhoto Kaka, he used to visit all our relatives regularly. He went everywhere on foot. Six or seven miles was nothing for him. He read stories of Tarzan, and then related them to me in Bengali.

Saroj had just finished his Matriculation from a school which had started only recently. Jotu was still a student there. When my mother heard it was a good school, she decided to put me in it. I was eight, but had not yet started formal schooling.

I am going to speak of my schooldays in due course, but I must mention here what I have always felt about holidays and the long break during Durga Puja. I used to look forward to these holidays with a great deal of eagerness, for it was only rarely that we spent these days at home in Calcutta.

I remember two holidays in particular. On one occasion, we were joined by my uncle and aunt and two cousins from Lucknow, my Chhoto Kaka and many other people from my family to go to Hazaribagh. We rented a bungalow called Kismet. Food was cheap and fresh, and the weather fine and invigorating. We climbed to the top of the Canari Hills, had a picnic in Rajrappa, and saw the falls at Bokaro. It seemed as if each day was wrapped in a golden foil of fun and laughter. The evenings, after dark, were spent in playing games by the light of petromaxes. What we played the most were charades. I believe members of the Tagore family also played the same game.

In this game, there have to be two groups. The first must choose a word, then use gestures to explain its meaning. The second group has to act as the audience and guess what the word is. A single word has to be broken down into several parts of make the 'acting' easier. The word 'carpet', for instance, can be broken into 'car+pet'; or 'butterfly' can be acted out as 'butter+fly'.

If it is a dumb charade, then one is allowed only to mime each word. However, if it is a talking charade, conversation between the players in the first group is permitted. They have to use the selected word in their conversation, as unobtrusively as possible. Only four scenes can be enacted for the audience to guess the word.

This game gets more interesting if there are a lot of people to play it. There were ten or twelve of us in Hazaribagh, so the evenings passed very quickly.

Another memorable holiday was spent on a steam launch in the Sunderbans. One of my uncles was the excise commissioner. His work took him to the Sunderbans at times. On this occasion, he offered to take several family members with him, including my mother and myself. We were joined by my aunt, four female cousins and a male cousin called Ranajit—Ronoda to me. Ronoda was a shikari. He took a rifle and a great many bullets. We were to go right down to the mouth of the river Maatla, through several canals and other waterways, and in the process travel across the Sunderbans. The whole trip would last a couple of weeks.

We spent most of our time sitting on the deck, taking in the scenery. Maatla was a very big river and it was difficult to see the other bank. The sailors would occasionally drop buckets into the water. When these were hauled up, many of them had translucent jellyfish in them. The scenery changed completely when our launch entered a canal. I could see rows of crocodiles stretched out in the sun with egrets sitting on their backs. They slipped back into the water as the launch got closer. The trees thinned out where the crocodiles were seen; and they were not very big trees, either.

On the other side of the canal, however, the forest was dense with huge trees. I caught sight of herds of deer a few times, but they, too, disappeared quickly as they heard the launch.

One day, we left the launch, got into little boats and landed in the forest, to look for an ancient and abandoned Kali temple. There were strange roots, sticking out of the ground like sharp, pointed spears. We had to pick our way carefully through these, leaning on walking sticks. Two of the men were armed, for tigers lived in this area. There was no telling when one of them might suddenly decide to make an appearance.

We did not see a tiger on this visit, but Ronoda did kill a crocodile. He asked the launch to be stopped when we saw a large number of crocodiles gathered near the bank. Along with three other men he took a small boat to get closer. We sat with bated breath for half an hour. Then we heard a rifle go off. The little group had travelled quite a distance. It took them another half an hour to return with a dead crocodile. It was skinned on the lower deck. Ronoda later had a suitcase made out of it.

A week later, we reached Tiger Point, where the Maatla joined the Bay of Bengal. The sea in front of us stretched to the horizon; to our left was a little island with a number of sand dunes. We bathed in the sea, which at this place was very calm, and spent a long time amidst the sand dunes. There could be no doubt that we had come a long way away from human habitation.

Memories of those days of pure joy, spent forty-five years ago in the Sunderbans, will always have a special place in my heart.

School

When does one's childhood end? I do not know how others might feel, but speaking for myself, I knew I had ceased to be a child the day I finished my Matric exams. I remember coming home, grabbing my schoolbook on mechanics and throwing it on the floor. Something told me that instant that I was not a child any more. I would soon be going to college, I was a grown-up now.

I am, therefore, going to finish talking about my childhood with an account of my schooldays.

I was eight and a half when I was put in a school. The same uncle who had once taken me to see a Bengali film took me to the Ballygunj Government High School. The class teacher of the class I was going to join (the fifth class, as it was known at the time; later it came to be known as class VI) wrote down a few questions for me, and gave me about four arithmetical problems. I was then taken to a different room to write my answers. I returned after a while to the same teacher, who was in the middle of an English lesson, and showed him what I had written. He glanced at it and nodded. That meant my answers were all correct, and I was admitted at once.

As I was taking my answer papers back, one of the boys in the class, called Rana, shouted from his seat, 'What's your name?' I told him. 'And what are you called at home?' he asked again. I had no idea how mischievous Rana was, or that it was not advisable to reveal one's pet name in school. So I told him innocently what I was called at home. As a result, none of my classmates ever used my proper name. 'Satyajit' was used only by my teachers.

My school was near the Beltola Road police station. On the other side of the road, to its east, was the David Hare Training College. Students undergoing the Bachelor of Teaching course from this college came to our school once a year to take some of our classes.

The school building was surrounded by a high wall. The sports ground lay on the southern end. An aerial view would have shown that the building was shaped like a T. The bottom half was the school hall, and the top was simply a row of classrooms. The chowkidar's room was on the right as one passed through the gate. On the left was a banyan tree. A cement platform had been built around its trunk. A large area under the tree was empty and barren, for that was where the boys played marbles during the lunch break. In the main ground, we played football, cricket and hockey. Our annual sports day was also held there.

If one went past the chowkidar's room, up a gravel path and then climbed three steps where the path ended, one would be on the long veranda that ran from one end of the building to the other. On its right were all the classrooms. Halfway down, on the left, was the entrance to the school hall.

The main event that took place in this hall every year was the annual prize distribution ceremony. Apart from this, the hall was used for lectures and a sit-down lunch on the day of Saraswati Puja. Once, two foreign actors came to enact a few scenes from *The Merchant of Venice*. We sat in the hall in folding chairs and watched a performance of Shakespeare for the first time in our lives. Suddenly, I noticed our English teacher, Brojen Babu, standing nearby, his eyes wide, his lips silently uttering the lines the two actors were speaking. Perhaps

he was simply testing his own memory, having read the play
years ago as a student.

One day (possibly once again on the day of Saraswati
Puja), we were shown a Charlie Chaplin film. The chowkidar
brought a notice to our class the day before to let us know when
the film would be screened. The teacher who was in our class
at that moment was a Mr Ahmed. We called him Ahmed Sir.
He took the notice from the chowkidar and read it out to us:
'Through the kind courtesy of Messrs Kodawk Company . . .'
He had not heard of the Kodak Company, so he probably
thought it was a Bengali name, the same as Modawk!

Steps went down from the top end of the veranda, beyond
which, under an awning, stood two tanks containing drinking
water. One had to bend low and cup one's hands to drink water
from the taps. Opposite the tanks, close to the wall, was the
carpentry class, where Mr Tarafdar ruled supreme. There were
tools of all kinds in this place. Hammers, chisels, saws and
fretwork machines abounded, and the room was always filled
with noises from various machines.

The bell hung on the veranda on the first floor, just above
the railing where the stairs ended. Only the chowkidar could
ring this bell. A cord had to be pulled to strike the bell with a
rod, but the bell swung round when the cord was pulled, so that

no more than one gong sounded at a time. How the chowkidar managed to make it ring properly remained a mystery.

The school office and the headmaster's room were on the first floor. The office had an almirah full of books, which acted as the school library. Three of those books—Sinbad, Hatemtai and Dagobart—were so popular that each of them had become worn and dogeared. All three belonged to the same series. Sinbad is still well known, Hatemtai is occasionally mentioned, but I cannot remember having heard of Dagobart since I left school.

Bookkeeping was another activity that took place in the office. A cylindrical ruler was rolled down ledgers to draw lines in red, blue and black, which was fascinating to watch.

The office and the headmaster's room were on the left as one climbed up the stairs. On the right was the staff room for teachers, followed by more classrooms. There were eight classes in all, from class three to class ten. There were about thirty students in each class. School began at ten o'clock. The lunch break was from one to two, after which classes went on till four o'clock.

When school reopened after the summer holidays, we had morning school for a month. The first class started at seven o'clock. In the light of the early morning sun, the classrooms looked quite different. Even the teachers appeared much less stern. Perhaps people get more and more bad-tempered as the sun climbs higher during the day. Morning school seemed much more quiet and peaceful to me.

Yet it would not be right to assume that all teachers were bad-tempered. In fact, if they punished anyone, it was almost always a handful of particularly naughty boys. The nature of the punishment depended on the teachers, or the gravity of the crime. Boys were cuffed, slapped, had their ears pulled, and some were told to remain standing on a bench, occasionally on just one leg. I cannot recall suffering any of these indignities myself, for I was generally known as a quiet and well-behaved boy ('goody-goody', said some).

The school had two headmasters in the six years I spent in it. The first one was called Nagen Majumdar. His son, Nonigopal, now writes for *Sandesh*. Nagen Majumdar looked exactly as I had imagined a headmaster to look like. He was of medium height, had a fair complexion, white hair, a thick white moustache, and was always seen in trousers and a jacket with high neck. No one had ever seen him smile. The boys referred to him as Noga. When the results of our final exams came out each year, the headmaster would visit all the classes clutching a list, and read out the names of those who had got the top three positions. I shall never forget the nervous palpitations the sound of Noga's approaching footsteps caused.

Nagen Majumdar was replaced by Jogesh Chandra Dutta. He was thinner than Nagen Babu, and his moustache was smaller. Nevertheless, he was well suited to the role of a headmaster. The trousers he wore were somewhat baggy. At that time, we were reading the story of Rip Van Winkle, which was a part of our text. In that story, there was mention of a certain type of trousers called galligaskins. These were worn by Americans four hundred years ago. We were all pretty impressed by the name of these trousers, but none of us had the slightest idea what they looked like. When Jogesh Babu arrived wearing baggy pants, we decided promptly that that was what galligaskins must have looked like.

Jogesh Babu was named Ganja by the boys, though I cannot remember why. It could be that Jogesh had first been shortened to Joga, and that got further distorted to become Ganja. We were all afraid of him, but one day, when he replaced an absent teacher and took one of his classes, we realized he was not as terrifying as we had thought. He told us many interesting things. His first question was, 'Where has the Bengali word *genji* come from?' We all knew a *genji* was a vest, but where could the word have come from? None of us knew that. Jogesh Babu told us, 'It is actually an English word—guernsey. Guernsey is a small island on the English Channel near France. Sailors there used to wear a similar garment. That's where the name came from.' Then he also told us about a long coat Bengalis used to wear in the past, called aulestar. This name was a distortion of ulster, an Irish province where this kind of coat was worn.

What he did next amazed us all. He went to the blackboard and wrote the Bengali numbers from one to nine in words:

Then he rubbed out each number partially. What remained, looked like this:

These were the same numbers, but in figures!

After this, Ganja seemed to grow much closer to us.

The teacher we revered the most after the headmaster was the assistant headmaster, Jyotirmoy Lahiri. We always called him Mr Lahiri instead of Jyotirmoy Babu, or Lahiri Sir, for no other teacher was as highly westernized as he.

Tall, handsome, clean-shaven and with a very fair complexion, he was always seen in a suit and tie. His jacket was just slightly short, but otherwise one could not find any fault with his appearance. When attending a function in the school hall, he always stood with his hands loosely resting on his stomach. If he wanted to clap, he never raised both hands. One of them remained fixed to his stomach. The other rose slightly, to strike the back of the other hand very gently.

Mr Lahiri spoke English with an impeccable accent. He taught us *Ivanhoe*. His pronunciation of the French names used by Walter Scott earned a great deal of admiration from the boys. After Jogesh Babu retired, Mr Lahiri became the headmaster. But, by that time, I had finished school.

Each of the other teachers had his own quirks. According to the rules laid down by the British government (who were still in power), there were a few Christian and Muslim teachers in my school, in addition to Hindus. Ahmed Sir was one of the Muslim teachers. His full name was Jaseemuddin Ahmed. He was the same man who had referred to Kodak as Kodawk. One of the other Muslim teachers who taught us was the poet, Ghulam Mustafa. He taught us Bengali for about a year. One of his poems was included in our text. Its first two lines ran thus:

> Deep in thought, lost to the world, went I,
> When in a small alley, I saw a little girl go by.

Mustafa Sir read the whole poem with great feeling. It became obvious that he was a simple man, and one of the mischievous boys in my class, called Gopal, could not resist making fun of him.

'Is it really true, sir?' he asked. 'This business of finding a little girl, I mean?'

'Yes, yes,' Mustafa Sir replied innocently. 'I really did see a little girl one day walk down a narrow alley. I tapped her little head as I went past.'

'You tapped her head? Good for you, sir!'

How this conversation might have continued, I cannot tell,

for at this moment a few other boys decided to intervene with 'Oy, Gopla, shut up, do sit down!' Mustafa Sir was then allowed to speak undisturbed.

We had two Christian teachers, BD Roy and Manoj Babu. BD Sir's initials stood for Bibhudan or Bidhudan. I have never heard such a name anywhere since those days. He was very particular about the correctness of English pronunciations.

Manoj Babu had a brother who was a police officer. He lived close to the local police station, which was practically next door to our school. Two of his sons—Sukumar and Shishir—were in my class. They always jumped over the boundary wall to get into the school. Sukumar was a very good runner; he won the hundred-yards race twice in a row. Shishir did very little except make mischief. He was punished almost every day, particularly by his own uncle. Manoj Babu did not like sitting in a chair while he taught us. He always stood leaning against his desk, with a book in his hand. He had a rather strange habit of lifting his right shoulder and tilting his neck at the same time, as if he was trying to get rid of a fly. He was also extremely absent-minded, and was given to saying 'very good' to everything, without even hearing what had been said. If any of his students said, 'May I go out for a minute, sir?' he would promptly reply, 'Very good.' Then, as we sat in silence, wondering what could be so good about wanting to go out, he would realize his mistake, grit his teeth and bark, 'You went out five minutes ago. Why do you want to go out *again*?'

There were two teachers who were referred to as Punditmoshai. One of them, the head Pundit, taught us Bengali. I remember him for his beautiful handwriting on the blackboard. I never saw another teacher with such good writing.

The second Pundit, for some obscure reason, was called Bhyan Pundit. This nickname had been bestowed upon him long before I joined the school, so its origin remained a mystery.

He, too, was a rather grave and sombre man, but not very good at controlling his class. I can still remember him shouting at us one day, saying, 'My throat has started bleeding from all the yelling I've done today, and you're *still* not paying any attention?'

He hardly ever raised his hand, but on one memorable occasion, he struck a boy called Ajay on the side of his head, which nearly made the boy lose consciousness. The news spread like wildfire throughout the school. The incident occurred before our lunch break, but no one left the classroom even when the bell rang. Ajay sat with a red face, clutching his head. The other boys stood surrounding him, and the teacher was more or less imprisoned in his class. Boys from other classes gathered outside the closed door, some jeering, 'Bhyan! Bhyan!' through the shutters. It was an event none of us ever forgot.

Some teachers used a different kind of weapon on a child. Instead of attacking his body, they attacked his mind by using words as sharp and wounding as an arrow. One particular teacher called Ramani Babu excelled in doing this. He had a permanent sneer on his face, and seemed ever ready to make a caustic comment. When we were in class eight, a boy called Sanjay joined our class. It turned out that he was related to the Tagore family in some way. Naturally, some of the boys started teasing him about this. To be honest, I had not been spared, either. It was generally known that I was Sukumar Ray's son and Upendra Kishore's grandson. Then, somehow, people came to know that the famous HMV singer, Kanak Das, was my aunt, and that the well-known cricketer, Kartik Bose, was an uncle. Soon after this discovery, boys started coming up to me, saying things like, 'I say, Manik, we hear King George V is your grandfather. Is that true?'

In Sanjay's case, the question he was asked a number of

times was, 'How are you related to Rabindranath? Are you his nephew or something?' There were two things that went against poor Sanjay. One was his complexion. Unlike other boys, he was extremely fair, with a pinkish glow to his skin. Apart from this, it soon became clear that he did not possess the artistic or intellectual brilliance the Tagores were famous for.

Ramani Babu realized this, and began taunting him almost at once. 'Come here, Mr Tagore. All glitter and no gold, eh? My, my, look at your ears. They've gone quite pink. Would you like me to work on them a little more, and make them even pinker?'

Even the toughest wilted under the pronounced sarcasm in Ramani Babu's words. But there were other teachers whom we liked, and found it easy to communicate with. Brojen Babu was one of them. He was seldom stern with us. If the noise in the classroom got out of control, he would simply say anxiously, 'Cease talking! Cease talking!' However, these words did not always bring the desired effect. On one occasion, Brojen Babu could take it no more. He singled out a particular boy and shouted, 'You, over there! Come here at once!'

Startled, the boy rose and began moving forward to go and stand near the teacher's desk. None of us knew how he was going to be punished. Perhaps he would be asked to stand in a corner. But, before Brojen Babu could announce his punishment, another boy got up and ran to him. 'Please, sir,' he pleaded, flinging his arms around Brojen Babu, 'forgive him, sir. Please don't punish him. Not today, sir!'

Brojen Babu was still looking cross. However, taken aback by this unexpected development, he faltered, 'Why? What's so special about today?'

'Merchant scored a century today, sir!'

Brojen Babu was once called on jury duty. It was a famous murder case, and no one selected to be juror could refuse to attend. Brojen Babu was therefore obliged to miss school occasionally to be present at the hearing. A zamindar had been killed in a most dramatic fashion. Apparently, his killer had injected poison into his body at Howrah station, despite the crowds. Much was being written about this case every day. Pamphlets were being printed and distributed at street corners. Each time Brojen Babu returned after a hearing, we badgered him for details. He, too, seemed perfectly willing to share his experiences with us.

*

Ballygunj Government High School did not have a uniform in my time. Some of us wore shorts, others wore dhotis. A few Muslim boys came wearing pyjamas. It was customary to wear shirts over dhotis. Those who wanted to show off used to raise their collars, particularly if they were good in sports. Some of the senior boys—Keshtoda, Jatishda and Himangshuda—were all good sportsmen, and they all went about with raised collars. Keshtoda had a distinct moustache and signs of a beard, which

made him look much older. He could easily have been mistaken for a young man of nineteen or twenty. We were younger than him by only four years, but none of us bore even a hint of a beard on our cheeks—nor could we even hope for it in the near future.

The master collar-raiser, however, was not a student but a teacher. He was our drill teacher, called Sanat Babu. I had been in the school for three years when he arrived. Droopy-eyed and with looks befitting a film hero, he wore shirts with such wide collars that they nearly touched his shoulders. When he raised them, he looked as if he was about to take flight. What is called PT today was then called drill. Two or three times a week, we had to spend an hour in the school ground. The drill teacher behaved like a military officer. He made us parade up and down, then got us to practise high jumps. We had to leap over a bamboo pole placed horizontally several feet above the ground. The teacher's command, 'I say ja-a-amp!' shot out at anyone who was caught hesitating. Perhaps he thought elongating the last word added more weight to his command. I was among the boys often instructed to 'ja-a-amp', for when I was quite small, I had had an attack of dengue, which had affected my right foot. I could never do well when it came to jumping and leaping.

What I was good at was drawing. That was why our drawing teacher, Ashu Babu, grew very fond of me as soon as I joined school. He was from East Bengal, and spoke with an accent, pronouncing 'j' as 'z'. A comment he made about me, more than once, was 'Shoityozit in name, Shotiyozit in deed!' I was never able to figure out what he meant by 'Satyajit in deed'.

Ashu Babu was a thin man, with a sharp nose, a thick moustache, long and slender fingers, and long, oily hair that hung from the back of his head. The front of his head was quite bald. He had been trained at the Government Art School, but he did not know any English. Most of his students were aware of this. So, every time a notice was brought to the class, the boys shouted, 'Sir, there's a notice, sir!' At this, Ashu Babu would take one look at the peon who had brought the notice, and quickly get busy with something. Then he would call out to the class monitor, 'Dilip, can you come here and read out the notice, please?' Dilip always came to his rescue.

One day, Ashu Babu saw one of my drawings and marked it '10+F'. The others bent over my desk, saw what he had written and asked, 'Why +F, sir? What does it stand for?' Ashu Babu replied gravely, 'F stands for First.'

Ashu Babu used to get very busy a few days before the annual prize distribution. He was always in charge of decorating the hall, and organizing an exhibition of the students' paintings. Among the other events that took place before prizes were distributed was a special event to which Ashu Babu and his art students contributed quite a lot. It was called musical drawing. It was held every year, and is possible that the practice began when the school came into existence.

On the stage was placed a blackboard and several pieces of coloured chalk. One of the boys would sing, and another would draw a picture on the blackboard to match the song. During the years I spent in school, I heard the same song every year. It was Tagore's 'The pure white sails flutter in the soft breeze/Never have I seen such a boat sail'. There was one particular boy called Hari who used to draw the matching scene. He was older than me by three years. He had an amazing control over both his hands and his nerves. It is not easy to stay calm in a packed auditorium and draw a picture swiftly, without faltering. But Hari passed this test each year with flying colours. In 1933, he took his Matric exams and left the school. Who was going to take his place? Ashu Babu wanted it to be me, but I was most reluctant for I suffered greatly from stage fright. If I was ever given a prize for something, the thought of getting up on the stage to collect it from someone important, and then walking back to my seat with dozens of eyes watching me, always filled me with terror. In the end, a boy called Suranjan was chosen to take part in musical drawing. The picture was the same: a boat with a white sail on a river, fluffy white clouds in the sky, and a setting sun, visible through the trees on the other side of the river. Suranjan did his best, but he lacked Hari's style and his sure, firm strokes.

Two other events became a regular feature at this function. They started three years before I left the school. The first was a tabla recital by Master Phulu; and the second was Jayant's magic show. Phulu was younger than me, but Jayant was older. Phulu had been playing the tabla from the age of seven. When he grew up, he began playing at bigger functions.

Originally, I was junior to Jayant by a couple of years. But having failed twice in the same class, he became my classmate. That he was going to fail his exams yet again became obvious when we sat for our finals. All of us saw that he kept glancing not at his answer sheet, but down at his lap. Why was he doing

it? Did he have a book open in his lap? Our invigilator noticed it too and came running to check. 'What are you looking at?' he demanded. Jayant raised an object and offered it for inspection. It was a large, ripe banana. 'I brought it to have during tiffin, sir,' he explained. 'I was just making sure it was still there.'

He had learnt magic when he was only about ten, and had practised regularly. He knew quite a few things, other than the tricks usually done on the stage. Only a few days after joining our class, a boy called Parimal suddenly became unconscious. It transpired that Jayant had pressed two points by the side of his neck, and Parimal had fainted. Jayant explained that what he had pressed were the carotid arteries. If those were pressed for a few moments, blood supply to the brain was reduced and a person could lose consciousness. But if the pressure was removed, he would regain consciousness in a matter of seconds.

Jayant also excelled in tricks that involved sleight of hand. But that was not all. We became aware of the full extent of his capabilities when a boy called Asit invited us all to his birthday party. Jayant was going to have a show after dinner. But, even before the meal was over, he took a glass of water, drank it, then began eating the glass! He learnt to eat glass and swallow nails before leaving school. But, only a couple of years after I finished school, I heard that Jayant had tried drinking acid, and died.

Another boy among my classmates deserves a mention. He was called Anil. There was something special about him. Anil had spent a few years of his childhood in Switzerland to recover from some serious illness. On regaining his health, he returned to Calcutta and joined our class in 1933. I was then in class eight. Just as Sanjay had a connection with the Tagores, one of Anil's relatives was a famous Bengali called Lord Satyendraprasanna Sinha. Anil had to take his share of teasing because of this. Once, during a history lesson, we were being told about the history of Rome. As soon as the teacher mentioned Etruria and Lars Porsena, a boy called Faroukh piped up, 'What did you say, sir? Lord Sinha?' Anil reached out and tapped Faroukh rather sharply on the head, but by then everyone had started laughing. Lord Sinha was, in fact, Anil's maternal grandfather.

Anil himself was quite a good student. Having lived abroad for many years, his Bengali was a bit shaky, but he made up for it by doing well in English and mathematics. He was the only son of a wealthy father, which meant that he could get things that none of us could even dream of. In those days, Nestlé had started a scheme under which they were enclosing pictures with their one-anna packets of chocolates. Each picture was a part of a series called The Wonders of the World. They were to be pasted in an album, also provided by the manufacturers. We began vying with one another to see who would be the first to fill a whole album. The problem was that there was no guarantee that the packet one bought would not have the same picture that had already been used. Anil had enough money to buy a hundred packets. It took him only a day to fill his album almost completely. He was very generous with his spare photographs and allowed other boys to have them, but it was naturally not

the same as finding a new picture from one's own packet of chocolates.

At a time when we wrote with nibs that had to be dipped into the inkwells built into our desks, Anil wrote with a Parker fountain pen. We were happy to use box cameras that cost five rupees. Anil turned up one day with a German Leica camera, worth at least five hundred. He also brought an enlarged photo of the tennis tournament held at the South Club. When yo-yos first became available, Anil bought eight of them. Later, many other boys were seen with this amusing toy. One day, Anil arrived with a pair of roller skates. He went out on the long veranda wearing these as soon as our lunch hour began and spent the whole time skating from one end to the other.

The lunch hour was spent eating and playing. Many boys brought lunch from home in tiffin boxes. My friends and I bought aloo-dum, which was wrapped in leaves and sold for one paisa each. It was just one whole potato, boiled with added spices. With it came a tiny stick, like a toothpick. The potato had to be lifted with the stick.

One day, we discovered that something new was being sold. Wrapped in paper, it looked like butter, but was actually an ice cream called Happy Boy. It was manufactured by an Indian company, who were among the first to use push-carts to sell ice cream. Very soon, Happy Boy began to be sold everywhere in Calcutta. In the course of time, it was replaced by Magnolia, and then came Kwality and Farrini.

Marbles were a popular game played during the lunch break. The other common game, played by many, involved spinning tops. A man called Gupi Babu, who was considered to be the best maker of tops in Calcutta, used to set up shop every evening on the steps just outside a bigger shop called Mitra & Mukherjee. Those who haven't seen him spinning tops cannot imagine how expertly it can be done. The boys in my school tried to hit one top with another to crack or damage it, send their tops flying in the air, still spinning, then catch it in their palm, swiftly transferring it from one palm to another. Once a flying top hit a boy's leg, which started bleeding profusely.

I can remember other accidents happening on our sports ground. Once, during our annual sports, a boy called Sushant got badly hurt. We used to have a race called blindfold race. Sushant, who was good both at studies and at sports, stood with the other runners with his eyes covered by a blindfold. They were to run a hundred yards. The race began. Sushant moved away from the line he was supposed to be in and began veering to the left. We could all see it, though Sushant himself was quite unaware of what had happened. Someone from the audience shouted out to him to warn him. Sushant stopped for a second; then, thinking he was losing valuable time, began sprinting even faster. Before anyone could say or do anything, he moved entirely off course and went and hit his head against the compound wall, fifty yards to the left of the finishing post. I can still feel a chill go down my spine whenever I think of the scene of his accident and remember the thud of his impact with the wall. Blindfold race was banned from the following year.

*

I remained in Shona Mama's house in Bokulbagan for four years after I started school. Then, when I was in class nine, he moved to Beltola Road, taking all of us with him. The new house was larger. Our next-door neighbour, Sudheer Ray, was the son-in-law of the famous freedom fighter, Deshbandhu Chittaranjan Das. Mr Ray owned a pale yellow car, which was the first Mercedes Benz I ever saw. He had two sons, Manu and Montu, who became my friends. Like his father, Manu went on

to become a barrister in later life, finally entering politics and
becoming the Chief Minister of Bengal. Everyone now knows
him as Siddhartha Shankar Ray.

Beltola Road had a local club. I was invited to join it as
soon as we moved there. Manu and Montu were members.
Another barrister called Nishith Sen lived only a couple of
houses away. They had a large playing ground where we played
cricket and hockey; in the smaller ground at Manu's house we
played badminton. Nishith Sen's sons and nephews—Chuni,
Phunu and Anu—were all members of the club. More members
came from Mr Chatterjee's house. They were Nilu, Bolu, Anath
and Gopal. I already had a number of friends from school who
came to visit me at home. They always stood outside, without
bothering to come in, and yelled loudly, 'Manik, are you
home?' Now, I could add all these boys from my
neighbourhood to my group of friends.

There was a boy called Arun at our club, whose pet name
was Panu. He went to the South Suburban School and was in
the same grade as me, although he was older by nearly four
years. It turned out that he had failed in his exams and had been
retained in the same class quite a few times. No one in the club
seemed to be close to him, possibly because he was considered

to be lacking in brains. But, one day, Panu joined the Dum Dum Flying Club and learnt to fly an aeroplane. Then he invited us to their annual day celebrations and startled us all by taking off in a two-seater plane, rising high in the air, then diving down towards us at great speed while making a great deal of noise, before shooting up in the sky once more. After this, all of us began to treat him with a lot more respect.

In those days, according to government regulations, no student under fifteen could sit for Matric exams. Our exams were to start in March 1936. I was then going to be fourteen years and ten months old. Technically, I could not take the exam and would have to spend a whole year twiddling my thumbs. How awful! If we went to a lawyer, he could probably help me change my age illegally, but my mother would not hear of it. Strangely enough, only a few months before the exams, this particular regulation was changed and the age restriction lifted.

Ten years after I left school, I had to return there on one occasion, possibly to attend an old students' reunion. When I entered the hall, I was amazed. Was this the same hall that had once seemed so large? Why, my head was touching the top of the door! And it was not just the door. The veranda, the classrooms, even the benches meant for the students—everything appeared much smaller than I remembered.

It took me a while to figure out why. When I left the school, my height was five feet three inches. Now, ten years later, it was nearly six feet five inches. Naturally, the school had not grown. I had.

I never went back to my old school. I know now that if one has fond memories of a place, going back there can seldom bring back old joys. It is far better to simply dip into one's fund of memories, and relive precious moments.

'Two and a Half Years with Apu'. Explaining the scene to Apu and Durga in the kaash field

Waiting for the clouds

Tea break. Ray with Apu

Apu and Durga enjoy a chat between takes

With Apu and Durga before a shot

Apu trying to look through the camera, standing on a stool

'Hundi-Jhundi-Shundi'.
Snow-covered Kufri
near Simla was Jhundi

...Then Hundi.
An unnamed spot
near Jaisalmer

Finally Shundi. This
scene was shot near
Bundi in Rajasthan

'The Army of the Raja of Halla'. The commander-in-chief climbs on to his camel and commands, 'To Shundi!'

The army in the front and in the distance, Goopy and Bagha are singing to mesmerize the soldiers

'Camels versus Trains'. The director waiting for the camera to arrive.
In the distance, the actors are ready on their camels

Feluda, Topshe and Jatayu who is nearly half dead, on their camels

'With Feluda in Varanasi'. Front door of Maganlal Meghraj's house

Steps going up to the palace from Darbhanga Ghat. Flocks of pigeons can be seen on the parapets

Feluda, in search of Machhli Baba's secret hideaway, has entered
the ruins of the Darbhanga Palace

Gyan Chakravarti's house in Nagwa—the Ghoshal residence
in *Joi Baba Felunath*

Ruku in *Joi Baba Felunath* standing with revolver in hand beside the
door to the room on the roof

Crowds waiting to watch the shooting at Darbhanga Ghat

Maganlal on his way to meet Machhli Baba

Returning to Dashashwamedh Ghat on the boat after completing
the day's shooting

Ray giving instructions to Topshe and Jatayu who are in disguise
in Darbhanga Ghat

Lalmohan Babu and Topshe on a rickshaw. The director is inside
the car with his eyes to the camera

Crowds beginning to collect in the gali where the scene with the bull was shot

Feluda and Topshe slip past the bull easily

Topshe, Feluda and Lalmohan Babu in Pandey Haveli's deserted gali

Ray testing the arrangements on the rickshaw which has been attached to a taxi

Shooting in front of Shri Ram Sweet Shop in Varanasi's famous Thatheri Bazar

Preparing for another shot in another gali of the same bazar. Cable lines are laid on the road and the camera is on the trolley

Ray on rickshaw with camera in hand

'Please, Please Bagh Mama'. The tiger expresssing its discontent fiercely
as soon as it is brought to the set

'Bagha remained frozen in that
position, his back arched
over the tiger, his
hands stuck to the wall,
as if he simply could
not straighten himself and
move away, even if he tried.'

Goopy continues to sing with Bagha beside him and the tiger behind him

Making Movies

Introduction

The entire business of making a film can be divided into three parts. The first is writing everything down, the second is filming it, and the third is joining the filmed pieces together.

What is finally shown on the screen is first written like a story. This is called a screenplay. When film-making begins, in accordance with everything that is written in the screenplay, it is done chiefly with the help of a camera and equipment for recording sound. This whole process is called shooting.

Once the shooting is over, the scenes that may have been taken haphazardly are arranged in the order in which they appear in the screenplay. What emerges when this task is done is what people see on the screen.

It is the shooting of a film that entails a lot of hard work and is the most difficult part of the job. Sometimes, it takes place not in a studio, but outside, in the natural environment.

In the last twenty-five years, I have had to travel to many places in the country to shoot some of my films; but I had to travel the most for three films in particular: *Goopy Gyne Bagha Byne, Shonar Kella* (The Golden Fortress) and *Joi Baba Felunath* (The Mystery of the Elephant God). This book describes some of the strange and wonderful experiences we had while shooting in a village in Birbhoom, in the alleyways and the ghats of Varanasi, the desert in far-flung areas of western Rajasthan and the snow-covered hills in Simla.

It is experiences like these that make all the hard work seem

worthwhile, particularly if one can overcome all hurdles and
finish the job successfully.

Two and a Half Years with Apu

The film *Pather Panchali* (The Song of the Road) was shot over two and a half years—although, naturally, we did not shoot every single day during that period. I was then working in an advertising agency. I could shoot only on holidays, or by taking time off from my work. We did not have a lot of money. When we ran out of what little we had, there was nothing we could do but wait until more money could be raised.

Finding suitable actors was a big task before the actual shooting could start. When it proved totally impossible to find a boy of about six to play the role of the young Apu, we had to place an advertisement in the papers.

A room was hired in Rashbehari Avenue in Calcutta. Every evening, boys of that age were brought there for us to look at. We saw a number of them, but none struck us as suitable. One day, a boy arrived with visible traces of talcum powder on his neck. This made me suspicious. 'What's your name?' I asked. 'Tia,' the child replied in a thin voice. 'Did you just have his hair cut?' I said to the man who had accompanied him as his guardian. He realized the game was up, and could no longer hide the truth. It turned out that the child was really a girl. Her guardian had had her hair cut and brought her to us, in the hope that she would get to play Apu's role in our film.

When no suitable boy could be found even after placing the advertisement, we were almost ready to give up. Then, one day, my wife, who had gone to the roof of our house for a while, climbed down and said, 'I saw a boy playing on the roof of the house next door. Why don't you call him?' Eventually, it was the boy from next door—Subeer Banerjee—who became Apu in our film. When we first started shooting, we did not, obviously, expect it to drag on for more than two years. As the months wore on, we began to worry that Apu and Durga might both grow up quickly, in which case the changes in their appearance would become obvious in the film. Luckily, neither grew as much as they might have. We were also deeply relieved that eighty-year-old Chunibala Devi, who played Indir Thakrun, remained alive until the film was completed, despite all the strain of shooting.

When we began, there was a problem at the very outset. Little Apu and Durga were taken to a place called Palsit, seventy miles from Calcutta, near Burdwan. Here, by the side of a railway track, stretched huge open fields filled with kash, a tall grass with white flowers found abundantly in Bengal. The scene to be shot was the one in which the two children see a train for the first time. It was going to be a lengthy scene, so we knew we needed at least two days to take all the shots. The first day was a holiday as it was Jagaddhatri Puja. We worked all day and managed to take half the shots required. The scene showed Apu and Durga having a fight. Then Durga ran away, and Apu followed her out to a kash-filled meadow. Everyone in the unit—the director, cameraman, and the two young actors—were all new, so at times people felt ill at ease; but there was no lack of enthusiasm. Having finished a day's work, we returned to Calcutta. We went back to the same place in Palsit a week later. But was it really the same place? Where had all the kash gone? It was barely possible to recognize the area. Some of the local people told us what had happened. Apparently, cows are very fond of kash flowers. In the past week, they had eaten all of it. It we took further shots here, they would certainly not match the previous ones.

The remaining portion of the scene had to be taken a year later, when the field was covered again by fresh kash. This time, we also took some shots of a train; but there were so many shots to be taken that we had to use three trains—one was not sufficient. A look at the timetable had told us at what time trains ran on that particular line. They had to come from the same direction; those going the opposite way would not suit our purpose. One of our team members, Anil Babu, was asked to wait at the station from which these trains started. He got into the engine with the driver, to make sure that the boiler was stoked with coal as the train got closer to the spot where we were waiting. This was necessary, as without a well-stoked boiler, there would not be enough smoke. How could the scene make an impact if we did not show black smoke against the white kash?

When seeing the film, it is impossible to tell that three different trains were used at three different times during the day. If we had to shoot the same scene today, when most trains use either diesel or electricity, we would not have been able to take those shots in the same way.

Running out of money and having a frequently disrupted schedule led to various other problems. Let me tell you about one of them.

In *Pather Panchali*, the novel, there is mention of Apu and Durga's pet dog, Bhulo. We had managed to find a dog in the village, which soon became quite friendly with all of us. There is a scene in the film which shows Apu's mother, Sarbajaya, feeding her son. Bhulo is sitting in the courtyard, watching Apu eat. Apu is sitting with a bow and arrow in his hand; his back is turned, and he is really not all that interested in eating. He is simple waiting to be allowed to go off and play with his bow and arrow.

He shoots his arrow even before he has finished eating. Then he gets up to go and fetch it. His mother runs after him, the plate in one hand, and a handful of rice in the other. But it is obvious that Apu is not going to eat any more. Bhulo, too, has got to his feet. His eyes are on the plate of rice.

The next shot was going to show Sarbajaya throwing away the remaining rice on a heap of rubbish, and Bhulo polishing it off. But this shot could not be taken on the same day that we took the previous ones. The light faded away, and so did the money in our pockets.

It took us six months to raise enough money. Then we went back to Boral (where the main shooting was taking place) to take the remaining shots. We learnt upon arrival that Bhulo was no more. He had died some time in the last six months. Now what were we going to do?

Someone said that there was another dog which looked very like the first one. All right, we said, get that dog.

Our informant, it turned out, was correct. The second dog looked remarkably like Bhulo. Not only did it have an identical brown coat, but the tip of its tail was also white, like the other one. In the end, it was this 'fake' Bhulo that was shown following Sarbajaya out, and eating all the rice from the rubbish heap. No one watching the film could ever make out that the two dogs were different.

But it was not just a dog that caused us problems. The same thing happened to one of our actors.

There was a scene that involved a sweet-seller called Chinibash. Apu and Durga could not afford to buy anything from him. So, in that particular scene, they follow him to the house of the Mukherjees, who are very rich and are bound to buy some sweets. Apu and Durga are happy simply to watch from a distance.

As in the scene with the dog, we ran out of money after

filming only half this scene. A number of months passed before we could resume shooting. When we were finally ready once more, and about to set off, word reached us that the actor who was playing Chinibash had died. Even if no one noticed the slight dissimilarities between two dogs, where were we to get another man who looked more or less the same as the first Chinibash?

The person we found eventually bore no facial resemblance to the dead actor, but was as plump as Chinibash number one. We took the remaining shots with him. In the film, you can see the first Chinibash emerging from a bamboo grove. In the next shot, Chinibash number two is seen passing through the gate of the Mukherjees' house, with his back to the camera. Many people have seen *Pather Panchali* more than once, but I have never heard that anyone was able to see through our little ploy.

Something else caused us a great deal of trouble while shooting the few scenes with the sweet-seller. It was, once again, Bhulo, the dog. One of the scenes shows the sweet-seller standing on the side of a pond. Apu and Durga are standing on the other side, near their house, looking greedily at the sweets the man has come to sell. But, when he asks them if they want any, they have to tell him that they do not. Chinibash then starts walking towards the house where the Mukherjees live. Durga says to Apu, 'Come on, let's go!' and the two start running.

It occurred to me that the scene would become more interesting if their dog, too, went with them. So, in the first shot, I decided to show Apu and Durga watching the sweet-seller standing near a wall, and the dog sitting under a guava tree. Durga would start running as soon as the sweet-seller left, followed by Apu who, in turn, would be followed by the dog.

We found the owner of the dog and told him to stand behind the camera, a little to the right. 'Call out to your dog as soon as you see Apu running after his sister. Do you think he'll move if you call his name?' I asked. The man gave me a smile, nodded happily and said, 'Oh yes, sir. You can test him, if you like.'

We decided to have a rehearsal. Everything went smoothly. The owner of the dog called out to it, and the dog responded at once. Good, there was nothing to worry about.

I started taking the shot. Durga began running, Apu followed suit, the dog's owner began calling out to his dog—once, twice, three times. The camera was still whirring, using up our precious film. A thousand feet of film at that time cost nearly a hundred and fifty rupees. In this shot we had already used up film worth at least ten rupees. But the dog simply glanced at his owner, then looked away, without moving an inch. Cut, cut, cut!

The camera was switched off instantly. Even then the dog remained quite unperturbed. He obviously had no idea how badly he had ruined our plans. Yet, we could not give up. If the shot could be taken properly, it would definitely seem that this dog was Apu and Durga's own dog, their precious Bhulo.

It now seems incredible, but that day that foolish and lazy dog spoilt as many as eleven takes, and nearly a thousand feet of film. The twelfth take, however, went exactly according to plan.

The following shots showed the sweet-seller walking through a bamboo grove. Apu was right behind him, and then Durga, and behind Durga was the dog. All were walking in single file. Nobody who saw the film guessed that the dog was behaving like an experienced actor only because Durga had clasped her hands behind her back, and in those clasped hands was a large sweet to tempt him along!

Lack of funds also stopped us from filming scenes in the rain. The monsoon came and went, but we could not do anything because we had no money. By the time we could get enough money again, it was October. On bright, sunny days in October, I began going to the village with Apu, Durga, other members of the unit and all the equipment, hoping fervently that it might rain. Even a small dark cloud in the sky made us gape, and wonder if it would, by some magic, spread all over and come pouring down.

Finally, one day, our prayers were answered. The sky was covered by thick, black clouds and it started raining in torrents. Durga ran to join her brother under a tree, both looking for shelter and hugging each other. She chanted a rhyme under her breath in the hope that that would make it stop raining: *Nebu pata koromcha / hey brishti, dhorey ja* (Lemon leaves, fruit and berries / stop at once, what rain there is). It was very cold on that wet October afternoon. I was looking through the camera, standing under an alkathene sheet, and could see that little Apu, whose torso was bare, was shivering in the cold. Once the shots were over, we got both children to drink warm milk with a drop of brandy in it to bring some warmth back to their cold and drenched bodies. It must be admitted that the scene turned out very well. Anyone who has seen the film, I think, would agree.

Boral proved to be ideal for shooting *Pather Panchali*. Apu and Durga's house, Apu's school, fields, ponds, bamboo groves, mango orchards—Boral and its surrounding areas had them all. Now, the village has got electricity, its roads are paved, and its houses are made of bricks and cement. Such was not the case in those days.

Since we had to visit the village a number of times, we came to know some of its inhabitants quite well. One of them was somewhat peculiar. We used to call him Subodhda. A man in his mid-sixties, he was quite bald, lived alone in a small hut, and was seen muttering to himself on the front veranda of his house. At first, when he heard that we were in the village to shoot a film, he was not at all pleased. He would shout the

minute he saw us: 'Look, those film people are here again. Grab
your spears and attack!' He was known to be slightly mad, as
we learnt later. In due course, however, he became quite
friendly. Sometimes, he even got us to sit on his veranda and
played music from old jatras (folk operas) on his violin.
Occasionally, he brought his face close to my ear and
whispered: 'See that man going on a cycle? Do you know who
that is? It's Roosevelt. He's a crook!' Other men were
Churchill, or Hitler, or Abdul Ghaffar Khan. Everyone was a
crook, each of them was a sworn enemy.

A washerman lived in the house next to the one we were
using. He, too, was decidedly eccentric. He was in the habit of
raising his voice and saying, 'Dear friends!' before following
that up with a long political speech. This did not matter at any
other time, but if he started a speech when we were working, it
seriously disturbed our soundtrack. This would have remained
a problem, if other members of his family had not helped us out.

The house we had chosen came to us in a state of great
disrepair. There were wild plants everywhere. The owner of the
house lived in Calcutta. We paid him a monthly rent for its use.
It took us almost a month to clear the vegetation and make
necessary repairs before we could start working.

There were several rooms in a row in one portion of the
house, which we did not show in the film. These were used as
storerooms. Most of our equipment and other paraphernalia
were stored here. In one of these rooms sat our sound recordist,
Bhupen Babu. We could hear his voice, even if we could not
see him. After every shot, we would shout: 'Is the sound all
right, Bhupen Babu?' He would then shout back his reply.

One day, the usual question after a shot brought no answer.
So I repeated it: 'What about the sound, Bhupen Babu? Is it all
right?' Still, there was no answer. What could have happened?
Most curious, I stepped into his room and saw a huge cobra
gliding down through one of the rear windows. The sight of the

snake had naturally rendered Bhupen Babu completely speechless.

We had, in fact, seen the snake before, within a few days of our arrival. We wanted to kill it, but the local villagers had told us not to. Apparently, it was an old snake, known to be living in that derelict and abandoned house for a long time. It was considered both improper and inauspicious to kill such a snake.

Project Tiger

No one can beat Hollywood when it comes to making films with animals in them. I remember films in my childhood—and there were quite a few of them—that had an alsatian called Rin-tin-tin. This dog's acting was more impressive than a human's. Later, we got to see three or four other films with a collie called Lassie. It seemed that the director could make Lassie do just about anything. These trained dogs were famous stars in their own right, and the money they earned was no less than what a real film star got. Their owners could easily make as much as a hundred thousand rupees from just one film.

I realized how reverently these animal-actors were treated when I happened to see the shooting of a film twenty years ago in Disney Studio in Hollywood. The main character in this film was a large dog, the kind that Americans call a 'shaggy dog'. I reached the studio to find that the shooting had not yet started; the cameraman was getting the lights ready. It is customary for actors to be present when the lights are arranged, for they have to show the cameraman how they'll walk, or where they'll stand, in a particular shot. In the case of very famous stars, this job is done by their stand-ins. A stand-in is usually a person who is physically similar to the real star. The stars themselves arrive only when the lights are ready and it is time to take a shot.

Here, in Disney Studio, I noticed that a few actors were moving about in the set, and on one side, standing quietly, was

the protagonist—the same large dog. The cameraman shouted
to everyone to take their positions. But the dog remained where
it was. This puzzled me. Could it be that it was not required in
the next shot?

Before I could ask someone, a strange thing happened.
From nowhere appeared a little dwarf, followed by another man
carrying a hairy dog-skin. Then, to my perfect amazement, the
dwarf went down on all fours on a chalk mark on the floor, just
like an animal, and the dog-skin was draped over him. Then he
crawled from one mark to another, and the cameraman got busy
with the lights. It finally dawned upon me that this dwarf was
paid to be the dog's stand-in!

Every animal in a Hollywood film is well trained. It is not
difficult to train a horse or a dog. But have you ever heard of
trained ravens? Not just one or two, but nearly a hundred of
them? Even this was made possible in Hollywood, when the
creator of some of the best suspense films in the history of
cinema, Alfred Hitchcock, decided to make a film called *Birds*.
In the story, birds from all over the world start attacking
humans. Hitchcock needed a variety of birds, but what was
required in the largest number was ravens. Notices were placed
in the press all over the United States, asking people to contact
the film-maker if they knew how to get hold of trained ravens.

Someone replied within a few days. He was asked to bring
his birds, and he arrived with almost a hundred trained ravens.
Admittedly, their training had not gone very far. That is to say,
they could not do anything that might be seen as extraordinary.
But if as many as fifty ravens are told to perch quietly in a row
on a specified spot, and if they obey this command instantly,
isn't that pretty impressive?

Needless to say, in our own country, it is not at all easy to
find trained animals, although some films have been made in
Bombay and Madras that involved working with elephants,

horses and tigers. Their performance did suggest that they were used to obeying commands. In Bengal, it is sometimes possible to find clever dogs, particularly police dogs which are quite intelligent. If one is prepared to be patient, it is not altogether impossible to get good performances out of them as we managed to do with Bhulo in *Pather Panchali*.

Yet, a dog might be difficult, but not impossible to handle. What was one supposed to do if there was need for a tiger in a film? We had to deal with this problem, too, when we were shooting *Goopy Gyne Bagha Byne*. The story of the film goes somewhat like this: Poor Goopy is ordered out of his village by the king. He is sent off on a donkey and ends up making his way to the forest where he must spend the night. There is every possibility of finding a tiger in that place. Nervous and apprehensive, Goopy gets off his donkey muttering, 'What if a tiger catches him in the forest, after dark? What if Goopy dies?' He finds a path running through the forest and is walking along it when he meets Bagha, who has also been banished to the forest. As the two begin a conversation, suddenly they see a tiger and freeze. But the tiger simply walks about in the forest, without paying them the slightest attention. Then it goes back in the same direction from which it had come.

Having thought of this scene, I simply had to shoot it. But where were we going to find a tiger? The obvious thing to do was to look in a circus, since they were likely to have trained animals. As a matter of fact, one called Bharat Circus was visiting Calcutta at the time, holding shows in Marcus Square. We sent someone to make an appointment with its Tamil manager, and then went to meet him one morning. This was my first visit to a circus at a time when the performers were all resting. We went straight to the manager's room—sorry, tent. I noticed several little tents on three sides of the main one. The manager's tent was quite large, complete with the necessary furniture and linen.

He greeted us warmly, and ordered South Indian coffee for us. It was made and served by some of the girls who rode horses or performed feats on the trapeze during the shows. The manager heard the reason for our visit, then sent for one Mr Thorat. He turned out to be the ring-master. He, too, was a South Indian, very well built, with features somewhat like those of a Nepali. He was perhaps no more than forty. He showed us an old scar on his forearm, which had been caused by a tiger.

We told him what we wanted. The shooting was taking place near Shiuri in Birbhoom. We wanted to show a tiger in a thick bamboo grove. All the animal was required to do was come out of the bamboo grove into an open space, pace gently for a while, look at the camera if possible, and then go back. Could a tiger from Bharat Circus do this job? Mr Thorat nodded. 'How long will you need it for?' asked the manager. 'Perhaps a couple of hours for the shooting,' I replied. 'But that would be in addition to the time it'll take to travel to and from Shiuri.' On being told that the travel itself should take no more than two days, the manager agreed to put the tiger in its cage, and send it in a lorry. For those two days, their show would have to do without the special item that needed a performance by the tiger.

Mr Thorat now got to his feet and invited us to take a look at the tiger. '*Aaplog aaiye, sher dekh lijiye,*' he said. We went with him behind the manager's tent. It became clear that a mini zoo had sprung up in Marcus Square. The animal that attracted our attention immediately was a hippopotamus. A tank had been dug for it in the ground which was filled with water. A lorry was standing by this tank with a cage in it. A stout plank came down from the lorry to the edge of the tank. When the circus finished its stint in Calcutta, the hippo would no doubt have to climb up that plank and get into its cage before being carted to their next destination.

There were many other animals, including a lion, a bear and different species of tigers. Mr Thorat pointed at a couple of Royal Bengal tigers and said he would take one of those to Shiuri whenever required.

'Do you think it's going to be easy to set the animal free into a bamboo grove?' I couldn't help asking.

Mr Thorat frowned. 'I'm not sure,' he replied. 'I have never let him out of his cage on his own, so really I don't know.'

What! Were all our plans going to go down the drain? How could we let the tiger's trainer be seen with the animal? How could Goopy and Bagha be petrified with fear if the supposedly ferocious animal was accompanied by a man? No, we could not allow that to happen.

Mr Thorat found a solution. 'I'll tie a wire round the tiger's neck. It will be thin, but strong.'

'Good idea. But you'll have to find a very long wire.'

'That's not a problem. The free end can be tied to an iron rod.'

If the wire was thin enough, perhaps it would remain invisible to the camera. But it was likely that the hair on the tiger's neck would be flattened by the wire, which would give the whole thing away. I thought for a while, then had an idea 'What if we found a collar made of tiger skin, fixed the wire to this collar and then tied it round the tiger's neck?' I said.

Mr Thorat agreed. We finalized everything in ten minutes. Mr Thorat was given the date by which he had to be in Shiuri, and was then paid an advance sum. 'Please do not worry, sir, everything is going to be all right,' he said reassuringly. We said thank you and goodbye to the manager. Just before we came away, the manager made one request: could we mention the name of Bharat Circus in the credit titles?

*

We spent quite a few days working near Shiuri and Rampurhat, shooting scenes all over that area. A village called Notun Gram had been chosen to show where Goopy lived. About fifteen miles from there, by the river Mayurakshi, we had found a suitable bamboo grove to film the first meeting between Goopy and Bagha, and the appearance of the tiger. We heard on the appropriate day that Mr Thorat had left Calcutta with his tiger the previous evening, and had reached the spot selected for our shooting. We went over quickly to join them. There were about twenty-five people in our unit. A few local people took our permission to go with us to watch how we tackled the tiger.

The cage on the lorry was covered. Mr Thorat removed the cover on seeing us. To our considerable surprise, we saw that he had brought both his tigers. Why had he done this? Surely one would have been enough? 'I decided to play it safe,' Mr Thorat explained. 'If one doesn't get it right, we can use the other.' Somehow, I did not like this at all. But I did not dare ask him what we might do if the second one did not get it right, either. So I simply told him to wait until we had got everything ready. The few tigers I had seen earlier in small circuses had been a pathetic sight, but the ones owned by Bharat appeared to be well fed and robust.

We mounted the camera on its tripod and placed it so that it faced the bamboo grove. Then Mr Thorat was told that we were ready for him. The audience was instructed to get behind the camera and stand as far back as possible. We had to stay relatively close to the bamboo grove, and Goopy and Bagha, too, had to be within yards of the camera, for it was necessary to have at least one shot that showed them together with the tiger.

While we were making our own preparations, Mr Thorat's men had fixed a five-foot iron rod to the ground, about thirty feet from the area where the tiger was supposed to take a walk.

Three-fifths of the rod had disappeared under the ground. Then they took a thin, long wire and fixed one end to the collar made of tiger-skin that the tiger was already wearing. The other end was tied firmly to the visible portion of the iron rod.

*

We were ready. The door of one of the cages was unfastened. Mr Thorat called out to the tiger. It responded almost at once and sprang out of its cage to land on the open space outside. What followed was totally unexpected. One look at Mr Thorat's startled and helpless face told us that he was as taken aback as the rest of us. Instead of walking sedately in a dignified manner, the tiger started prancing around with tremendous enthusiasm. It leapt, it jumped, it rolled about, dragging its poor trainer, who was desperately clutching the wire tied to the tiger's collar in a futile attempt to bring it under control. We stood around foolishly, watching a new and strange kind of circus which we were getting to see for free! The camera was still standing on its three legs, staring into the wood, but the tiger was showing no sign of making its way there.

After nearly five minutes of madness, the tiger finally calmed down a little. Mr Thorat and his two assistants looked a sight. The ring-master spoke through pale lips and explained that this particular tiger had never been in the wild. It was born in a circus and had seldom been released from its cage. A sudden taste of its natural habitat had probably gone to its head.

Once the tiger had calmed down, we managed to take the few shots we needed. However, another unforeseen problem then arose. The door of the cage was now standing wide open. A stool had been placed near the lorry. The tiger was supposed to jump on the stool when its trainer said, 'Up!' and then run into its cage, so that the two assistants could then lock the door once again. Mr Thorat went blue in the face saying 'Up!' but the tiger ignored him completely. Instead of returning to its cage, it seemed far more interested in sitting in the bamboo grove and tasting the young leaves on a stem.

Mr Thorat had clearly never faced such a situation before. But the tiger's behaviour made us feel quite reassured, even bold. A tiger that chewed bamboo leaves could definitely not be a man-eater. I took the camera even closer to the tiger and used the remaining film to capture this most un-tiger-like behaviour. However, purely out of the blue, even as the camera was running, the tiger shot up in the air, took a giant leap, and got back into its cage. It must have covered the distance between the lorry and the bamboo grove (a matter of at least sixty feet) in just about a second.

This should have been the end of the story. But, when we returned to Calcutta and looked at the scenes with the tiger, we realized that our camera had failed to work properly. The shots were too dark, so much so that the tiger was merging almost completely with the background of trees and leaves.

What were we going to do now? Should we admit defeat and drop this scene from the film? Oh no. Bharat Circus had not left Calcutta yet. We went back and spoke to Mr Thorat again. A brave man, he agreed to give it another go. The good thing was that this time, he and his tiger did not have to travel as far as Shiuri. We had found another bamboo grove closer to Calcutta in a village called Boral. Boral was well known to us, for we had shot most of *Pather Panchali* there, working with Apu, Durga and Indir Thakrun. Now, we would have Goopy, Bagha and Mr Tiger.

The lorry arrived once more, with Mr Thorat, the tiger, the steel wire, the special collar and the iron rod. And with the lorry came the whole village. Every single inhabitant—big or small, young or old—was eager to watch the shooting. The memories of our previous experience with the tiger were still fresh in our mind, so we told the villagers not to come close to the camera. They should stand at a distance of at least seventy feet, even if it meant not getting a good look at what was going on. Once the film was released, they could easily see what shots were taken.

No one paid any attention to what they were told. The entire crowd moved as close to the camera as they could. We could not afford to waste any more time explaining and arguing. So we got the camera ready, and signalled to Mr Thorat. Goopy and Bagha had taken their positions. Mr Thorat opened the door of the cage.

What followed was perhaps something never ever seen before. The instant the door opened with a clang, our tiger emerged with a loud roar, and charged straight at the villagers gathered behind the camera. On the first occasion, we had seen the tiger disappear from the open wood into its cage in a matter of half a second. This time, before our eyes, the crowd, consisting of about a hundred and fifty people, melted away as if by magic. Quite literally, it was there one moment, but gone the next. The tiger could not get very far, for its trainer had pulled it back by its collar, but of course no one knew that was likely to happen. I don't think I shall ever forget the speed with which so many people vanished at once, or the look of sheer terror on their faces.

Strangely enough, after that great burst of energy, the tiger calmed down very quickly. Like an obedient child, it walked over to the spot we had chosen, paced about quietly just as it was required to do, and then ambled back to its trainer.

Even the camera behaved this time, which we realized two days later, when we returned to Calcutta and saw the scenes we had shot.

Hundi-Jhundi-Shundi

Goopy and Bagha had been blessed by the king of the ghosts, who had given them three boons. The first enabled them to get whatever food or clothes they wanted, at any time, any place. The second enabled them to travel anywhere in the world, if they put on their magic slippers, also given to them by the king. All they had to do was join their hands and clap together. The third boon turned the tone-deaf Goopy into a gifted singer, and Bagha became an accomplished drummer.

Anyone who has seen the film *Goopy Gyne Bagha Byne* knows what happens next. The two men clap their hands and get a lot of delicious food by magic. Just as they finish eating, they see a singer of classical music, an ustad, go by in a beautiful palanquin, followed by his whole entourage. Where are they going? One of the men tells Goopy and Bagha that they are going to a place called Shundi, where the raja is holding a music competition. The ustad is going to take part in it.

A few seconds after the departure of this group, it occurs to the two men that there is nothing to stop them from going to the same competition. If the raja likes their music, they may be appointed as his court musicians. Thanks to the slippers given by the king of the ghosts, going to this place is not a problem. But, wait a minute. What was the name of the place? Neither Goopy nor Bagha can remember. Goopy thinks the man said 'Jhundi'. Bagha is convinced it was 'Hundi'.

After arguing for a while, Bagha agrees to clap his hand

together with Goopy's, both shouting 'Jhundi!' In a flash, they find themselves in the land of ice and snow. Shivering with cold, their teeth chattering, the first thing they do is clap again and ask for warm clothes. Then they start fighting. Jhundi clearly was the wrong place. 'All right, let's go to Hundi,' says Goopy.

A second later, they are in the middle of a desert, their warm clothes nearly killing them. As they begin to peel them off and throw them away, both of them remember the correct name of the place. It was Shundi.

In the film, this whole sequence runs for three to three and a half minutes. Today, I am going to tell you about the experiences and the problems we had in filming these scenes.

*

The first few scenes of the film were taken in a village called Notun Gram in Birbhoom district. These included the first good meal Goopy and Bagha have together, the arrival of the ustad and the first clap as they say, 'Jhundi!'

As soon as they do this, both men are seen leaping up and vanishing into thin air. We had to work quite hard to make this happen. An eight-foot-high bamboo machan was built. Then we placed the camera below it. Goopy and Bagha were asked to use a ladder to climb on to the machan and then jump down so that they landed before the camera. While filming this particular shot, we had to make sure that the film in the camera ran in reverse motion. We knew that when this was re-run and played normally, the pictures on the screen would be the reverse of what the camera had captured. The two characters would therefore appear to fly off in the air instead of jumping down to the ground.

The next scene would show them away from the river, the trees and the fields in their village. They would be surrounded only by snow. Where could we go that would give us enough snow? We learnt eventually that if we went to Simla in February, there might still be a great deal of snow left. And eight miles from Simla, a thousand feet further up, was a place called Kufri. All it had was snow, there were no houses or any other signs of habitation. We decided to shoot the few scenes with Goopy and Bagha in Kufri, and so set out from Calcutta to travel to Simla via Delhi. A few members of our team stayed on in Delhi, for on our return we were supposed to go to Rajasthan where scenes showing the two kingdoms of Shundi and Halla had to be shot. The group that went to Simla and Kufri was relatively small, consisting of about ten people including the two actors.

*

I had been to Simla once before, but that was during the summer. Now it was difficult to recognize the place. It seemed as if the whole city had developed a skin disease. There were thick white patches everywhere—in the streets, on the houses, on the hills, even the branches of trees. Some of the snow on the streets had started to melt, making the surface extremely slippery. Every step had to be taken with caution.

We did not have much time, so we left in a taxi soon after lunch to look for a suitable spot in Kufri. The following day, we would have to return with all our paraphernalia to this chosen spot. Apart from the camera, we would have to carry the eight-foot-high machan. This was a different machan, made of steel instead of bamboo. At the end of this scene too, Goopy and Bagha had to be seen shooting off into the sky, so it was necessary to have them jump off the machan once more.

Although it was just a matter of eight miles, it took us nearly an hour to get to Kufri. The road we took was under eight inches of snow. It clung to the side of a mountain and there were several sharp twists and turns. The wheels of our taxi had to cut through this snow. Occasionally, the tyres got stuck so deep, that although they spun furiously, spraying snow in every direction, they could not actually move forward.

The sky had been overcast, but soon after we reached Kufri, the sun came out. Kufri was really a village, where facilities had been built for people who came here for skiing in the winter. There was a club, a bungalow and a rest house. We needed none of those, so we began looking for a suitably barren and snow-covered region. It had to be reasonably close to the main road, or we would never be able to reach it with all our luggage.

We climbed another two hundred feet and came to an area that was totally exposed on three sides. When we looked around, all we could see was a range of mountains, each covered with thick layers of snow. A white hill rose on our right. We stopped the car and climbed out. In spite of all that snow, it was not very cold. As a matter of fact, when the sun came out, it felt quite pleasant.

Suddenly, it started snowing again, although the sun was still shining. A fine powdery curtain wafted down from the sky. If one stretched a hand out, one's palm turned white in a couple of minutes. The snow fell in absolute silence, which added a touch of mystery to the whole thing. Besides, it was very strange to see something fall from the sky, although there were no heavy clouds.

There was no time to be lost. We began exploring the area, despite the fine flakes of snow, and finally found what we wanted. About ten feet above us, there was a natural platform on the hill, where Goopy and Bagha could stand quite easily. I decided immediately that that was where they should arrive, straight from their village in Bengal. There was nothing visible in the vicinity except snow and dark rocks that occasionally peeped out of it.

*

We had found the right spot, but now we had a different problem. In the last scene, Goopy and Bagha were still in their village, wearing short dhotis and kurtas, with just a light cotton shawl draped over their shoulders. When they land on the snow, they must be shown wearing the same clothes. But it was too cold here. What were we going to do? The two actors playing Goopy and Bagha were so full of enthusiasm that they said it did not matter, they would jump on the snow clad in their ordinary cotton garments. But the rest of us thought this was taking things a bit too far. So, in the end, it was decided to give them sleeveless pullovers which they could wear under their kurtas. In order to cover their legs, they were given nylon stockings. The colour of these stockings merged with the colour of their skin, so it was not possible to tell from a distance that they had them on. Apart from these, on their feet were the magic slippers. These had been specially made for the film.

To make sure that the scene was truly effective, we decided to show the two characters jumping about in the snow with the cold and eventually slipping and rolling down the hillside. The two actors, as eager as ever, agreed readily to do what was required. But, although I liked the idea, when I thought it over, I began to get a little worried. After all, they had never rolled down a snow-covered hill before. What if they got hurt? There might be hidden rocks and boulders, who knew?

As we were discussing this matter among ourselves, we were overheard by one of the local residents. He came forward to offer us reassurance. Apparently, the particular area we had chosen was quite plain, free from rocks and stones that might be jutting out of a hill. The man appeared to be speaking with conviction and seemed reliable. So we decided to go ahead with our plan.

When the camera was ready, Goopy and Bagha climbed up the hill, placing their feet on the rough surface of the rocks that were still visible, and soon reached the platform. I started the camera. Needless to say, there was no time for a rehearsal. Luckily, we could get all the shots we wanted in just about five minutes.

You may remember having seen the two figures rolling about in the snow in the film. But you cannot possibly know what happened when the shot was over. The two stars scrambled to their feet and announced, 'We have lost our slippers!' What! How? When? 'Just as you started taking the shot,' they replied. Both pairs had slipped off their feet as they began jumping. They were now lying buried under the snow.

We spent the next thirty minutes digging the snow to look for them, but they were lost for ever. They would probably be found in the summer when the snow melted away. We felt quite amused to think of the possible reaction of the local people if they did find two pairs of dark slippers, with huge big eyes of ghosts painted on them.

Anyway, things might have been worse. Fortunately, we had had the prudence to get an extra pair made for both of them, so the loss of the first pair did not really matter.

The following shots went very well. Trembling in the cold, Goopy and Bagha clapped and asked for warm clothes. Immediately, they were given woollen Tibetan dresses. We had got these from a European in Calcutta. Bagha lost his temper as soon as he was a little warm. He began throwing great handfuls of snow at Goopy and shouted, 'Jhundi? Is this your Jhundi? Is this where that competition is being held?' Shamefaced, Goopy was obliged to say, 'Very well then, let's go to Hundi.'

The steel machan had been erected on the snow. Goopy and Bagha went through the same motions, climbing the machan and jumping off on the snow, to give the same effect of taking flight. And that was all. We had finished shooting in Kufri. Now it was time to travel to the deserts of Rajasthan.

*

The only real desert in our country is the Thar, which is in western Rajasthan. But there were other places that we had to visit. In the story of *Goopy Gyne*, as you may remember, there are two kings. One is the good king, who rules in Shundi. The other is the bad king, whose kingdom is called Halla. For the former, we had chosen Bundi. There are few places in Rajasthan that can match the beauty of Bundi, with its trees and flowers, fields and lakes and hills. For the bad king of Halla, Jaisalmer had been chosen, which was the opposite of Bundi. Beautiful it was, yes, but its beauty had a harshness in it. It was almost totally barren.

Even so, the real desert was not in Jaisalmer. To find it, we were told to travel twenty-five miles further west. We left one day with Goopy and Bagha to see if we could find an appropriate place in the desert where they might arrive straight from the land of snow.

It did not take us long to leave Jaisalmer behind. We drove on for a mile, crossed a nullah full of stones, and reached an area where no vehicle except a jeep could move. This did not worry us for we had anticipated this and had hired a jeep, but it was not always keeping to the paved road. The general demeanour of our driver suggested that either he knew this region like the back of his hand, or he did not know it at all, which was why he was going simply where his fancy took him.

Perhaps he had enough confidence in Allah to believe that He would get him to his destination.

Gradually, I noticed that the traces of sand in the ground appeared to be diminishing. Every ten minutes, one of us asked the driver, 'Where is the desert?' And each time he replied, 'We'll find it.' All we knew was that we had to reach a place called Mohangarh. The term 'garh' automatically made me think of a fort, so I was quite interested. More so, because no book I had read on Rajasthan had mentioned a place called Mohangarh.

We drove on for another ten or twelve miles, and found ourselves in a place where there was no road to speak of. It was not just the road that had disappeared. With it had gone the trees, the houses, the hills, and even the little mounds that were visible a while ago. And the sand? The sand, too, had vanished completely. I had travelled pretty widely in our country, but never before had I seen such a place.

Then the scenery began to change. One minute we were going through a rocky terrain, where there seemed to be nothing but stones and pebbles; the next minute we were passing through heaps of broken earthenware; and then we were surrounded by what looked like endless pumice stones! None of these areas were flat. Our jeep had to negotiate quite a few bends and curves and slopes. No matter where we looked, the landscape looked as if it consisted of huge, unmoving waves. It was a strange sight. However, this was not what we wanted. We had to have a proper desert. How else could we show the contrast between snow and sand, or suggest that Goopy and Bagha had gone from a terribly cold place to a terribly hot one?

Allah saved the day, and we eventually found Mohangarh. Yes, there was indeed a 'garh', but it was a small, modern structure, not in the least like the other forts of Rajasthan. It aroused amusement, rather than awe. Still, we could not come away without seeing it from the inside. So we stepped in, and found that classes for children were in progress in the open courtyard. We did not have to be told that no battle had ever been fought here.

We had travelled for twenty miles, and yet there was no sign of the desert. Was the entire trip going to be a complete waste? The money we had spent on petrol, the time we had spent, the bumps and jerks in the jeep we had suffered?

Finally, a local man in Mohangarh told us what had gone wrong. We had taken the wrong route right from the word go. The desert was in a different direction altogether. As I stood trying to come to terms with this revelation, the driver of our jeep made a brave suggestion. Since we *had* come all this way, he said, it would not be wise to go back without looking around a bit more. Why didn't we travel further west? If we still did not find what we were looking for, he would take us straight back to Jaisalmer.

Very well, we agreed to set out once more. This time, only a mile later, I saw a place that—strictly speaking—was not a desert, but I knew I could not find a better place for the scene I had in mind. If this place had a name, we never learnt it. Here, there was plenty of sand, but not the wavy sand dunes one associates with a proper desert. The sand stretched tightly on a flat surface for as far as the eye could see. If one walked on this surface, one realized there was water below it. There were, however, patches of dry sand, of a paler hue than the rest. The afternoon sun fell directly on this land, its light reflecting in the sand and dazzling our eyes. It was not particularly warm in late February, but when seen through our camera, I had no doubt that this stretch of sand would seem no different from the Sahara.

I got the driver to stop as soon as I saw this place. The sudden joy and excitement at having found exactly what I was looking for made me feel quite breathless. Then I happened to glance westward and, for a second, my heartbeat seemed to stop. Where *were* we? No one had told us there was such a huge lake in Rajasthan. It was, in fact, large enough to be called an ocean, but the water was absolutely still, there was not even the hint of a ripple. We could all see the water clearly, right up to the edge of this sandy stretch. There were reflections in it of the few clouds in the sky and, on the right, in the far distance, a row of trees. We stood speechless for a few seconds. Then it dawned on us that what we were seeing was not a real lake, but a mirage. Rarely did one get to see such a perfect mirage in the desert.

It did not take us long to set up our camera and shoot the one-and-a-half minute sequence showing Goopy and Bagha's arrival and departure from the desert. When we returned to Jaisalmer in the evening, many of the local people said they knew about this mirage. Sometimes it fooled not just men, but also animals. Every year, herds of thirsty deer begin walking in that direction in the belief that they would find water. Each of them die eventually, without finding a single drop.

Camels versus Trains

Those who have seen the film *Shonar Kella* (The Golden Fortress) will know that there is a rather interesting episode in it involving camels. The writer of crime thrillers, Lalmohan Ganguli alias Jatayu, has often dreamt of riding a camel in the desert. Towards the end of the film his dream comes true in an extraordinary manner. The villain, Mandar Bose, who is being pursued by Feluda, manages to ensure that the detective's car gets a puncture, not once but twice, thus foiling his plans to get to Jaisalmer by road. Stranded in the middle of nowhere, Feluda and his companions spot a group of Rajasthani men riding camels. Feluda decides to take a lift on those camels to the nearest railway station which is at Ramdeora, eight miles away. They can then catch the train to Jaisalmer which calls at Ramdeora at midnight.

Feluda and Topshe have nothing to worry about. Both are young, smart and used to regular exercise. But Jatayu? Faced with camels in real life, his dream quickly turns into a nightmare. What strange animals they are! Dim and droopy eyes like drug addicts, large, uneven teeth, chewing some mysterious object all day long. And when they move, they sway so much that it seems as if every bone in the body of the rider would come apart. If he has to climb one of these creatures, heaven knows what misfortunes might lie in store.

But there is nothing Jatayu can do. Feluda and Topshe spring up on the camel's back with no problem. Lalmohan Babu tries, nearly loses his balance, but somehow manages to hang on. '*Chaliye ji,* Ramdeora!' Feluda says to the leader of the group.

As they start moving, with Lalmohan Babu still feeling terrified, Topshe suddenly sees a train in the distance. If the train can be stopped, they can save themselves a ten-hour wait at Ramdeora. The camels start running towards the train and soon reach the railway line. Feluda takes out a white handkerchief from his pocket and starts waving it anxiously, in the hope that the driver will see him and stop the train. But that does not happen. The driver ignores him completely, and the train simply whooshes past, whistling loudly. Feluda grits his teeth and says, 'Shabaash!' By this time, Jatayu is half dead. This is an experience he is never going to forget. The group makes an about turn and resume their journey to Ramdeora.

This, basically, was the sequence that had to be shot. Now, if I describe the problems we had to face to shoot just these few scenes, you will get an idea of what an elaborate process film-making is.

*

Everyone knows there is no dearth of camels in Rajasthan. While making *Goopy Gyne Bagha Byne*, we had to get hold of one thousand camels in just two or three days. For *Shonar Kella*, our need was much less. But the problem was that the place we had selected was far removed from any kind of habitation. As far as the eye could see, there was only an expanse of sand, dotted with thorny bushes and dried grass. A meter gauge line cut across the desert, seemingly without a beginning or an end. A motorway to Jaisalmer ran parallel to the railway track. Had it been further away, we could not have shot a single scene here. We were based in Jaisalmer and our crew had to bring all our luggage to this chosen spot. The cameraman had to get into an open-topped jeep with the camera in order to catch the camels running towards the train. It was essential therefore to have a paved road nearby.

We had to travel the hundred miles from Jodhpur to Jaisalmer and search every inch of the way before we found this place which seemed most suitable. It was about seventy miles to the east of Jaisalmer, in the direction of Jodhpur. The camels had to be brought from a village called Khachi, seven miles further east. The owners of the camels were told to dress them well. We may well laugh at the appearance of a camel, but to a Rajasthani, a camel is his best friend, sometimes the only thing that can keep him alive in the desert. So, from ancient times, they have shown this animal a lot of affection by dressing it in colourful embroidered sheets, tassels, and even jewellery. When they move in a row across the desert, in all their finery, they seem to merge beautifully with the harsh and dry landscape. No other animal would have fitted in as well into the desert landscape as these ones. The owners said they would reach the spot by afternoon. It was agreed that some of our men would wait for them there, or they would find it impossible to locate the exact area.

We had got the camels, now we had to get a train. The one we had decided to use ran in the morning from Jodhpur to Pokhran. Pokhran was between Jodhpur and Jaisalmer. The exact spot where the shooting was to take place was twenty miles to the west of Pokhran, but we were more or less confident that the authorities would allow us to take the train where we needed it.

*

As we were getting ready for the big day, something happened that nearly destroyed all our plans. Suddenly, the price of coal went up, and the train we were going to use was cancelled at a day's notice. What a disaster! I had written this particular scene so carefully. Were we now going to have to drop the idea of showing Feluda and his team running through the desert on camels, trying to stop a train? No, we could not allow that to happen.

I met the railway authorities the same day, and explained that if this scene could not be shot, the main purpose of our visit to Rajasthan was going to be defeated. Fortunately, some of the officials I spoke to were sympathetic. They understood our problem and found a solution. They offered to give us a whole train, complete with six carriages, the guard's cabin, a coal tender and, of course, an engine. All we had to do was pay for the coal used. Oh, what a relief it was to see this problem so easily solved! In fact, it turned out to be a blessing in disguise for now the train was entirely at our disposal, at least for a few hours. We could make it start and stop, or run backwards and forwards, just as we liked.

It was decided that the train would wait for us at Pokhran. We would travel to Pokhran from Jaisalmer (a matter of a hundred miles) by car and board the train which would then leave for the spot in the desert where Feluda, Topshe and Jatayu would be waiting for us. On our way to this spot, we would take a few shots of Mukul (the little boy who wants to see the golden fortress) and the second villain called Barman (who has kidnapped Mukul, assisted by Mandar Bose). The scene would show the two inside the train—Barman nodding off, and Mukul staring out of the window, deeply engrossed in the scenery.

There was something else I wanted to show in my film. If I could get inside the coal tender, I could take a shot of the engine. It would be quite easy to get a close up of the engine's chimney, ejecting thick black smoke. Through this smoke, I could show the two railway lines running parallel to each other, stretching right up to the horizon.

The first hitch occurred at Pokhran. The train that was supposed to arrive at half past eleven, turned up at half past two. A delay of three hours meant complete chaos, especially when even a short delay of fifteen minutes could throw our carefully planned schedule out of gear. However, there was no point in wasting any more time arguing, so we picked up our luggage and got into the train.

The few shots with Mukul and Barman went off quite smoothly. Then the train was stopped so that I could get into the coal tender with two of my assistants. There was nothing here except a great mound of coal. I stood on this mound, camera in hand, and told the driver to start the train. He had a companion, who was the stoker. His job was to pick up pieces of coal with a huge shovel, and load them into the boiler. This kept the fire going which, in turn, helped a steady column of smoke hiss out of the chimney.

I stood on the mound of coal, my elbows pressed against the roof of the engine for support. In my hand I held the camera. As I was peering through it, my feet slipped now and then and I kept losing my balance. At first, I was greatly puzzled by this; but when I had finished taking the final shot, I realized that because I had been standing right on top of the mound the poor stoker had had no choice but to dig the coal from under my feet. Now I could fully understand the true meaning of the saying 'the rug was pulled from under my feet'!

We reached the site for the shooting to find the actors and the remaining crew waiting anxiously. The only thing that had failed to wait for us was the sun. It had started to set already. By the time we got the camera ready, it would undoubtedly disappear completely. There was no way we could shoot this precious scene in the fading light. There was nothing we could

do, except pack up and go back home. But it was agreed that
the following day, we would all return to the same spot at half
past two, including the camels. The train would also arrive here
without stopping at Pokhran.

*

As I have mentioned already, we were based at Jaisalmer.
About half a mile from the famous golden fortress, we had
found a small palace that was now being used as a guest house.
It was large enough to accommodate the whole unit, which had
nearly thirty-five people. The next morning, we rose early and
went straight into the fort to shoot the last few scenes of the
film. Then we returned to the guest house for a quick lunch,
before going back to the same spot as the day before. We got
there by half past two to find that the camels and their owners
had already arrived. Now we only had to wait for the train to
turn up. One look at the sky told me that the postponement of
our shooting was another blessing in disguise. The sky was now
flecked with grey and white clouds. Golden sunlight, streaming
through the gaps in the clouds fell on the desert, thereby giving
us a light that was suitably striking for this dramatic scene.

The train, too, arrived most punctually. We could not, of
course, help feeling anxious until it did, for we all knew that
this was our last chance to shoot the scene. It was essential for
us to return to Jodhpur the next day to leave Rajasthan and go
back to Calcutta in the evening. When at last we heard the train
huffing and puffing on its way, a collective sigh of relief went
up from the entire unit.

The driver saw us and stopped the train. We then explained
what was required of him. He would have to go back a quarter
of a mile. Then he would have to come forward again to meet
us. We would start our camera as soon as the train came into

view, and get the camels to start running with Feluda and team on their back. The open-topped jeep would wait on the road with the camera in it, and move alongside the camels.

The driver seemed to understand everything, except what had not actually been spelt out. As a result of this, our first attempt to take the shot failed rather miserably. As the train got closer, the camels began their run, and with them ran our jeep. Then they reached the railway line and Feluda took out his handkerchief to wave at the driver. With a squeal of the brakes, the train stopped almost at once. 'Why did you stop?' we asked the driver. 'Why,' he replied innocently, 'that Babu just waved his hanky and asked me to stop, didn't he?' The poor driver did not know the story of the film, so obviously had no idea what a difference his action would make to the following events. Anyway, we had to get ready for take two. Train, go back. Camels, go back. Jeep, go back. Start again. This time, everyone knew what had to be done. There should not be any problem.

The train reversed for a quarter of a mile and started again. There it was . . . we could hear it coming . . . it was almost within view . . . camels, get ready. A group of men were about to start pushing the jeep. The first attempt had made them break into a sweat. They were bracing themselves for the second.

I opened my mouth to say, 'Start camera!' but the words froze on my lips. The train was coming, yes, but where was the smoke? The whole idea was to show the glowing desert landscape disappear momentarily behind a thick layer of smoke from the engine. How else would the scene be interesting and exciting? Stop, stop, stop again . . . train, camels, jeep. We had to start all over again.

Every member of the unit left their position and rushed forward to stop the train, their arms raised high. *Roko, roko*!

The train squealed to a stop once more.

What had happened to the smoke? The stoker made a

confession. He was so busy watching the shooting that he had forgotten to put enough coal in the boiler. No wonder there was no smoke. Okay, but this time we could not afford another mistake. The light was just right. If we had to make a fourth attempt, it would be gone. I decided not to take any chances, and got one of our own men to join the stoker.

Feluda, Topshe and Jatayu mounted their camels once more. There was one advantage in taking the same shot three times. I knew none of the actors would have to pretend to be tired and uncomfortable. Jatayu already looked as if all he wanted to do was go home. Nevertheless, each of them wanted the shot to be perfect, so they were all prepared to ignore their personal discomfort.

Luckily, everything went according to plan the third time. We ended up with a shot that was perfect in every way.

However, this did not mean that our work was over. We still needed the train later that night at ten o'clock, to shoot another scene showing the railway station at Ramdeora. The train to Jaisalmer would arrive in the middle of the night, and Feluda, Topshe and Lalmohan would get into it. As the train started to move, Mandar Bose, dressed as a Rajasthani, would run and grab the handle of their compartment.

But that is another story.

The Army of the Raja of Halla

I have already spoken of the problems we had to face with shooting just a few scenes that had camels in them in *Shonar Kella* (The Golden Fortress). The number of camels we had to deal with on that occasion had only been five. But, a few years before that, for *Goopy Gyne Bagha Byne*, we had to get hold of a thousand camels to film a march by the army of the Raja of Halla. That was not all. We had to get a thousand men as well, and their costumes, shields, spears, flags, even naagras. To tell the truth, we had never worked on such a large scale before. So the memories of making *Goopy Gyne Bagha Byne* have become something rather special to whoever was involved in it. I am going to tell you now about some of our experiences.

When I wrote the screenplay of the film, based on Upendra Kishore's story in *Sandesh*, I was not sure of the place where most of the film might be shot. All I knew was that the soldiers in the Halla army would be on horseback. When I reached Jaisalmer in Rajasthan, I felt immediately that I could not find a better place to show the kingdom of Halla. But there were no horses in Rajasthan. The local people could only provide camels. So the army on horseback had to become an army on camelback.

Of course, simply replacing horses with camels in the screenplay did not mean the end of my task. If anything, it was just the beginning. A great deal had to be planned, and preparations had to be made. First of all, costumes for the soldiers had to be designed, starting with the turbans on their heads to the naagras on their feet. The commander-in-chief had to be given a slightly different costume, with additional armour and a different headdress.

Once these had been designed, a company in Bombay was ordered to make a thousand pieces, since a large army could hardly be comprised of fewer soldiers. This company was an old and established one, and specialized in making costumes for films. They agreed to pack all the clothes in trunks on a specified date, and load them on four lorries. We could start shooting only when these lorries reached Jaisalmer from Bombay.

*

Having sorted out the dresses, we now had to look for the soldiers and their camels. It was true that camels were a common sight in Rajasthan. But how were we going to get a thousand of them, together with their owners, on a particular day, at a particular time?

Eventually, we decided to consult the Maharaja of Jaisalmer. His palace was visible from Jawahar Nivas, the guest house where we were staying. I made an appointment with him and then went to see him, accompanied by a few other members of our unit. The man did not look like a raja at all. At least, his appearance bore no resemblance to the picture of a traditional Rajput ruler. He was not tall and hefty, nor did he sport a large moustache and beard. But it soon became clear how powerful and influential he was. 'A thousand camels? That's not a problem!' he said. 'Kumar Bahadur will get them for you.'

We had already met Kumar Bahadur. He was a distant cousin of the maharaja. A man in his mid-twenties, he went about riding a motorcycle, which made a lot of noise and left a

cloud of dust and sand in its wake. He was already excited about
the prospect of a film being made in Jaisalmer. When we told
him what we needed, he agreed readily to find us a thousand
camels.

The army of Halla is shown in just one scene in the film,
although that one is packed with action. The army has been
called to attention because the Raja of Halla has declared war
against Shundi. When the scene opens, every soldier, and his
camel, is sitting on the ground. Their commander shouts: '*Oont
uthao!*' (Get your camels on their feet!), but the raja's evil
minister has been starving the soldiers so they ignore the
command and continue to sit on the ground. The commander
runs post-haste to the minister to report the matter, who, in turn,
appeals to an old sorcerer called Barfi. Barfi has enough power
left in him to cast a spell on the army which makes them forget
their apathy and get on their camels at once. However, just as
they are about to march off to Shundi, Goopy and Bagha arrive
on the scene unexpectedly and begin singing. The army halts
in its tracks, and as soon as the song finishes, they see the sky
filling with endless pots of sweets. These slowly come down to
settle on the ground and the hungry soldiers pounce on them,
all thoughts of battle forgotten. Even the minister tries to grab
a pot and disappear with it, but in the general mêlée, he is
trampled by some of his own men, and his pot breaks. Goopy
and Bagha seize this opportunity to capture the Raja of Halla
and fly off with him to Shundi.

An excellent spot had been chosen to the east of the fort in
Jaisalmer where the army was to congregate. A wide expanse
of sand stretched to the horizon, without the slightest trace of
greenery anywhere. The sand was firm enough to walk on,
unlike other places in the desert where one's feet sank with
every step. To the north rose a steep rocky hill, spreading for
about a mile, forming a natural wall. The top of this hill was

plain. The Bhati Rajputs had built their fort on the top in the eleventh century. Hills like these—called table mountains—are to be found in many places in Rajasthan. Like the fort in Jaisalmer, the castle and the town in Chittor are also built on the flat top of a mountain.

Near the main spot selected for the shooting, there was an ancient burial ground for Rajput warriors. Spread over two hundred yards there were memorial pillars of various sizes, all made of yellow sandstone. When I saw this, I decided to show Goopy and Bagha walking here, singing one particular line from their song that speaks of the futility of war.

Soon, the day of the shooting dawned. Word reached us fairly early in the morning that a thousand men with their camels had gathered in the chosen spot. Each of us heaved a sigh of relief. The costumes had arrived two days ago, and we had arranged the dresses and the weapons separately. These were now sent over to the soldiers in the battlefield, two miles from Jawahar Nivas. A rough calculation told us it would take them about five hours to get dressed. Only ten people from our unit could be spared to make sure the soldiers were properly attired. The rest came with me to shoot a few other scenes in the morning. We thought we would start filming the scene with the soldiers at two o'clock. It would give us four hours to finish our job, for it was the month of March, and the sun would not set before half past six.

The total number of people in our team was around forty. Among the actors, in addition to Goopy and Bagha, were the Raja of Halla (Santosh Datta), his minister (Jahar Roy), the commander-in-chief (Shanti Chattopadhay), a spy (Chinmoy Roy), and five royal guards (Kamu Mukherjee, Ashok Mitra, Rajkumar Lahiri and others). Apart from them, there was a cameraman, a sound recordist, a make-up man, the production manager (all with assistants of their own), and men to carry light reflectors, cameras and sound equipment. I myself had four other men to assist me, which made a total of about thirty men.

With the exception of Jahar Roy, the rest of the unit was already in Jaisalmer. Jahar Roy had some other commitment in Calcutta, but he was going to join us the day before his presence was required, travelling all the way from Jodhpur in a taxi. We were expecting him to reach Jaisalmer at around ten o'clock at night. He turned up at half past two in the morning. What took him so long? He had had an accident, he told us. His taxi had overturned. We could see that his nose was injured. How did that happen? 'Purely by chance,' he explained. 'It was a lovely night, a beautiful moon in the sky, the road was good, and there was no traffic on it. We were going at sixty miles. The driver—a Sardarji—stretched his left arm out to rest along the front seat, picked up an apple with his right, and bit into it. He kept his paunch just below the steering wheel, holding it quite steady, but wiggling it a little, if need be. So there we were when, suddenly, a rabbit appeared out of nowhere in the middle of the road. The driver tried to swerve, but lost control. I rolled out of the overturned car, but remained conscious. After a while, I noticed two holdalls rolling with me. This surprised me since I knew I had brought only one holdall. Then I looked closely and realized that the second one was the Sardarji!'

The strange thing was that the driver, Jahar Babu and the car, all survived without any serious damage. So Jahar Babu did not find it too difficult to take part in the scene with the army the next day.

*

There was a tremendous amount of work to be done, so every pair of hands was needed. Each member of the unit—barring the actors—began making preparations from 4 a.m. onwards.

Had this been a Hollywood film, or even a film made in Bombay, there would have been at least three hundred people to take care of a scene involving a thousand men. But we only had about thirty. All of us knew that if we could get to the location by half past six and start shooting at seven, we would have the whole morning to finish our work. The light in the morning and in the evening is the best for photography, so we could not afford to lose a second.

Today, however, we had decided to shoot the easy and straightforward scenes in the morning for we knew how taxing the big scene in the afternoon was going to be. We returned to Jawahar Nivas at twelve o'clock for an early lunch and a short rest, before going to the battlefield at two.

The camels and the men were all waiting for us. The appearance of the camels was most satisfactory. We had asked the owners to dress their camels, and they had adorned them with jewellery, some of which were made with cowrie shells, and colourful sheets draped across their backs. No, I could not find fault with the camels. But the soldiers in the army? The same could certainly not be said about them. They were all still wearing their ordinary everyday clothes. What happened to all those red, blue and yellow garments? Those fancy turbans? And those thousand pairs of naagras we had bought for them? Why were those not on their feet?

A few questions revealed the whole story. Most of these men were Muslims, and they preferred wearing white. In fact, some of them had strong objections to bright colours. A few had simply laughed at the specially designed clothes that had come all the way from Bombay, some had frowned darkly and shaken their heads; and others had picked them up and cast them aside. Now what were we going to do? How could we explain to these men the seriousness of the situation?

To start with, how could we speak to a thousand men at the

same time? Then we remembered the battery-operated loudspeaker, for which we had paid three hundred and fifty rupees. It had been brought from Calcutta, knowing that we would have to work in an open area with a large number of people. Many of you may have seen this object. It is usually slung over one's shoulder. When the battery is switched on and the speaker, which looks like a huge funnel, is held close to the mouth, one's voice is greatly amplified.

It was time to call Tinnu Anand. He was one of my four assistants and had come from Bombay. He could speak fluent Hindi. A quick learner, he had already picked up quite a bit of Bengali. But now I needed him to address the soldiers. I handed him the loudspeaker and told him what he must say to the assembled men. 'Tell them they have not come here simply as owners of these camels. They are here as soldiers, and they are about to march off to attack their enemy. Their camels look beautiful, and their commander is dressed in all his finery. Now, shouldn't the rest of them be similarly dressed in colourful clothes? How else will they look the part they are playing? After all, when the film is released, they will be seen as brave warriors, not as simple village folk. They have to remember that.'

Tinnu took the loudspeaker and moved away to stand facing the men. Then he placed the speaker before his mouth and began speaking. '*Bhaiyon*!' he said, his voice booming across the entire assembly. But, after just that one word, there was complete silence. I turned hurriedly to find Tinnu still speaking into the loudspeaker, making gestures as if he was some sort of a political leader, but his voice could not be heard. The battery was clearly not working. Tinnu had not realized it, since he could hear himself speak perfectly well. This did not surprise me, for I had seen it happen to others earlier. If you can hear your own voice, it is natural to assume others can, too.

The loudspeaker had to be abandoned. The whole unit split into small groups to go and speak personally to all the men. After a while, our appeals began to take effect. A handful of men got up to change into their costumes. Gradually, the others followed suit.

Our first job was to picturize the song. The army was supposed to remain perfectly still when the song began. I noticed that some young men in the front row were getting restless. They were promptly dispatched to stand at the back. The old and the middle-aged men were chosen to stand in the front. We had to get all the camels in a proper formation, or they would never look as if a battle was about to begin. So we gave them another fifteen minutes to get into position; then the shooting began.

In order to film a song that went on for four and a half minutes, we needed to take at least forty shots, each of which was going to take about fifteen minutes. Some of them would focus purely on the soldiers, some would show Goopy and Bagha, and the rest would show both the soldiers and the two men. The song would be played on a playback machine. Goopy would sing along, his lips matching the words, and Bagha would play his drum. The camera, too, would move in keeping with the rhythm of the song.

We managed to take all the shots we needed in three hours on the first day. That is to say, all the shots leading up to the pots of sweets wafting down from the sky. The actual showering of sweets was going to be shot the next day. The men and their camels would spend the night in Jaisalmer, and we would bear their expenses.

Before I go on to describe the scene with the sweets, I must mention something else that happened on the first day. Everyone worked until the last possible minute before sunset, then started to get ready to go home. The soldiers were taking off their colourful costumes and getting back into their own, their plump commander (played by Shanti Chattopadhay) had dismounted from his camel to check if all his bones were in place, when suddenly the strangely beautiful sound of a flute reached us. A quick investigation revealed that the flautist had come with all the other men, though he had not bothered to don a costume.

Wearing a turban on his head, and a black waistcoat over a white shirt, the man had a quiet, faraway look in his eyes. From the pocket of his waistcoat were peeping not one, but two flutes. He was accompanied by another man, whose appearance was rather remarkable. He was dressed similarly, but was much taller than the flautist, probably over six feet. The colour of his skin was almost jet black, with an amazing polished texture to it. Under his sharp nose sat a most impressive moustache. I don't remember having ever seen anyone with such a complexion, or such a moustache. It rested on his cheeks, coiled two and a half times, like the springs of a giant clock. I learnt later that if it was uncoiled and straightened, its length measured nearly three and a half feet!

We told the flautist we had truly enjoyed what little we had heard. Would he care to come to our guest house later in the evening and play some more? I wanted to use his music in my film, if I could. The flautist readily agreed. His name, we learnt, was Shaukat Ali.

At around half past seven, he arrived at Jawahar Nivas with his friend. He sat on the carpet in my room and played for an hour. We recorded what he played. He startled us at the very outset by taking both his flutes out of his pocket and holding them to his mouth. As he blew into them, I realized we were in for an extraordinary experience. All but one of the holes in the first flute had been closed with blobs of wax. Out of this one would come a single steady note, a bit like a shehnai. The other flute had no obstructions, so that all the other notes could be played on it. I learnt later that these flutes were called satara. They had originated in a small village called Khuri, twenty-five miles to the west of Jaisalmer and only twenty miles from the border of Pakistan. Everyone in this village was poor, but all were exceptionally gifted singers and musicians. The flute of a snake-charmer—the been—had also originated in this village. It is now played virtually everywhere in the country.

When we had finished recording, Shaukat Ali turned to me with a strange look in his eyes. 'My only brother crossed the border and went to Pakistan,' he said. 'If you can play this tape on the radio, who knows, maybe he will be able to hear my music?'

*

While Shaukat Ali was playing his flutes, his friend was sitting quietly in a corner. He appeared to be a totally harmless fellow. Intrigued by the size of his moustache, we began chatting with him when Shaukat had finished.

When he revealed who he was, our eyes nearly popped out. He was a Bheel, and had once been one of the most ruthless dacoits of Rajasthan. His name was Karan. 'There's nothing left of my former strength,' he told us. 'There was a time when I could lift a jeep on my shoulders. Twice, the police arrested me. Each time, with these bare hands, I parted the iron rods on the window of my cell and escaped. But when they caught me the third time, do you know what they did? They drew a lot of blood from my body. Two bowlfuls. How could I remain the same when the main source of my strength was taken away from me?'

Seven years later, I met him again when I went back to Jaisalmer to film *Shonar Kella*. I failed to recognize him at first, for his moustache was no longer coiled and he seemed thinner than before. I learnt from him that Shaukat Ali had gone with his flutes to Pakistan. But it turned out that this erstwhile dacoit could also play a flute. It was totally different from a satara and was called naar. Its origins were in the same village called Khuri. A naar was nearly three feet long. What made it special was that the flautist did not just blow into it, but he also made a noise in his throat. The notes that rang out from the flute and the sound that came from the player's throat were both deep and sonorous. It created a rather eerie effect. Apparently, like the satara, this particular flute could be played by just this one single person in the whole country. One needed extremely powerful lungs to create this kind of music.

So much about music and musicians. Let's now go back to the battlefield in Halla.

The last few lines of the song, which were going to be filmed on the second day, had Goopy singing,

> Come, come, one and all
> bowls of sweets
> from the sky do fall . . .

The spell that had rendered the soldiers immobile would be broken as soon as Goopy stopped singing, and the sky would slowly fill with great pots of sweets. We had to use trick photography to show them coming down to earth, but this was done in a studio in Calcutta. I am not going to reveal how it was done, or it will spoil all the fun. Let me tell you what happened in Halla.

Food in Jaisalmer is not plentiful, but what is easy to get hold of are sweets made of kheer. About a hundred earthen pots were made to order, and were filled with such sweets. They were then placed in a line a hundred yards from the first row of the soldiers.

The first shot would show the soldiers looking at the sky. This would be followed by shouts of 'Mithai! Mithai!' They would then jump off their camels, rush towards these pots of sweets and fall upon them like hungry wolves. One shot would also show the gluttonous minister, trying to find himself a whole pot, but being jostled this way and that by the men who had dispersed and were now running wildly.

When we began explaining the shot to the soldiers, yet another weird problem arose. We were under the impression that all of them were Muslims. Now, it turned out that many of them were Hindus. As soon as they heard that the action involved eating out of those pots, they demanded that the pots be arranged separately, for no Hindu would eat from the same pot as a Muslim, and vice versa. Some of the men went a step further and said they did not like eating sweets, anyway. Now, this was something we could do nothing about. None of us knew how anyone could be made to eat sweets—and look as if they were enjoying it—if they were not fond of the stuff at all. So, those who declined were told to go home. Then the pots were divided into two sections. The Muslims were shown which was theirs, and the Hindus were told which ones they might eat from.

Finally, the arrangements were complete. Then something else happened. Just as I was about to take the first shot, purely out of the blue, a jeep drove up and parked bang in the middle of the open area where the soldiers were supposed to pounce on their sweets. Good heavens, it was the Maharaja of Jaisalmer! He had come with his wife and his pretty little seven-year-old daughter to watch the shooting. The maharani was sitting at the back, behind a screen. The maharaja was sitting next to the driver, his daughter in his lap. I was obliged to go and explain the situation to him. He had chosen the worst possible spot from which he could watch the tamasha. If he did not move his jeep at least thirty yards to the south, we could not work at all. Luckily, the maharaja understood the problem. His jeep moved away at once, giving us the space we needed.

*

Even after all that, I was not entirely happy with one thing. It is one thing to eat sweets every day. But it is quite another to find an endless number dropping down from the sky, especially if one has been deprived of even a single square meal for days on end. In order to produce a convincing show of being starved, desperate and greedy for more, we had to have proper actors. Since we were not sure of the acting prowess of the Rajasthani men, a few of our own actors (particularly those reputed to possess a large appetite) were quickly made up and dressed to look like the other soldiers and planted amongst them.

The men you have seen in the film stuffing their mouths eagerly were chiefly from our troop. One of them—Kamu Mukherjee—managed to polish off nearly a whole pot of sweets that day, all by himself.

With Feluda in Varanasi

The last time it had been Apu. This time I was back in Varanasi with Felu. I had visited Varanasi twenty-two years ago to shoot *Aparajito*. The little lanes and alleys of the city, its temples and ghats, its priests and holy men, and even its cows and monkeys were all shown in the film through the eyes of young Apu. This time, although it was the same place, the events were quite different. The city of Varanasi had to act as a backdrop to a mystery. Feluda, the detective, comes here on holiday, but gets involved in solving first a theft, then a murder. Varanasi had to be viewed with entirely different eyes.

It is very difficult to explain the special features of the city to those who have never been there. Calcutta has a ghat too; and alleyways in Shyambazar, Bagbazar and Borobazar. But those in Varanasi have a character of their own. They are unique to the city.

Take the ghats, to start with. There is no end to them, starting from Asi Ghat in the south, to Raj Ghat in the north. Their names and the buildings that stand by their sides give an idea of the city's varied past. For instance, Harishchandra Ghat in the southern end is one of the two big cremation grounds in Varanasi. Raja Harishchandra, in ancient times, had sold his wife and son Rohit to a Brahmin and spent a whole year as a slave to a chandal. Not far from here is Tulsi Ghat. Tulsidas had written *Ramcharitmanas* while living in a house near this ghat. To the north of Tulsi Ghat is the palace of Raja Chait Singh, which stands near Shibala Ghat. When Warren Hastings came to arrest him, Chait Singh is said to have jumped out of a window in his palace straight into the Ganges to save his life.

Many other rajas had their palaces built by the side of these ghats, so they have been named after the rajas. Mansarovar Ghat was built by Maharaja Man Singh of Amber; Rana Ghat by the Rana of Udaipur; and Ahalya Ghat by the Maharani of Indore, Ahalyabai. The famous Man Mandir on Man Mandir Ghat was built two hundred and fifty years ago by Maharaja Jai Singh of Jaipur. But the best known among all the ghats are Manikarnika, which is the oldest cremation ground in Varanasi, and Dashashwamedh, where Brahma was supposed have held ten *ashwamedh yajnas* (horse sacrifices). This ghat can be easily identified by its famous large umbrellas. Their handles go through a hole in a stone that is kept on the wooden seats used by the priests who are called pandas. These umbrellas stay propped against the stones, and can be moved as the sun changes its position, so that they can provide shade and shelter throughout the day. I have never seen such umbrellas anywhere else.

Among the lanes and alleys, the best known is the unbelievably narrow Vishwanath Gali. This alley, which is only about four feet wide, leads out of Dashashwamedh Ghat and winds its way to the temple of Vishwanath with its golden spire. Shops line both sides of this lane, selling every conceivable item. But two other things that Varanasi is famous for—rubri-malai and bronze utensils—are available elsewhere, the first in Kachauri Gali, and the other in Thatheri Bazar. It is possible to walk to other lanes from the temple of Vishwanath without actually going back to the main road. Many of the alleyways in Varanasi do not get any sunlight at all, at any time of the year. Large houses, several stories high, called havelis, are often found in these dark and dingy lanes. Most houses have an open courtyard at their centre. If you stood there and looked up, you would see the sky, a square blue piece on top of the building. If it wasn't for this, every room in the house would have to be artificially lit even during the day. It was in a lane like this that Maganlal Meghraj—the villain in our film—lived. So we had the job of finding a suitable house for him.

More than a hundred and fifty thousand Bengalis live in Varanasi. Most of them are to be found in a neighbourhood called Bangalitola. One hears Bengali being spoken so frequently in the streets, and so many shops carry signs written in Bengali, that sometimes it seems as if one is visiting a town in Bengal. Many of these families have been in Varanasi for as many as ten generations, and yet they speak Bengali without the slightest North Indian accent. The Mitters of Chaukhamba, for instance, are said to have lived in Varanasi for four hundred years, from the time of the Mughal rulers. They hold Durga Puja in their house, which is the oldest puja in the city. Their house is also in a small lane. It is impossible to tell from outside how big and sprawling the whole building is.

*

Feluda was supposed to roam the streets and ghats of Varanasi while he solved the mystery of the missing Ganesh, a little figure made of gold studded with a rare diamond, and the murder of a man. We went to Varanasi for three days to get an idea of where we night shoot, how good or bad the light was in those areas at certain times during the day, and whether the local people there would give us their support. The last was absolutely essential, so we had to speak to some of the residents.

The events described in *Joi Baba Felunath* (The Mystery of the Elephant God) take place over the five days of Durga Puja. The figure of Durga plays an important role in the story, so we knew we had to have a clay figure made in Varanasi. As a result, the first thing we did was to look for the potters who live in Ganesh Mohalla in Bangalitola.

Here I must stop for a second and describe the crossing at Godhulia, for one of the four streets leading out of Godhulia goes straight to Ganesh Mohalla. Just as Calcutta has its famous crossing at Shyambazar where five streets meet, or the big crossing at Dharamtola and Chowringhee, Varanasi has Godhulia. If you go there at a time when people have emerged from their houses to go about their business, you will find a solid wall at this crossing that is both mobile and noisy. Sometimes it seems as if each of the eighteen thousand cycle rickshaws Varanasi possesses has turned up here. The average pedestrian has very little chance of walking through this wall that is made not just of cycle rickshaws but also of endless people, tongas, cars and bicycles. Just occasionally, a few policemen in red turbans become visible in this human and vehicular ocean. They do wave their arms about every now and then, but no one pays them any attention. The police themselves hardly ever take their job seriously, for loads of things happen right in front of their eyes—cars hit cycle rickshaws, which in turn go and hit bicycles or pedestrians—without causing so much as a ripple. No one seems bothered by these minor mishaps, least of all the police.

We managed to drive down the street that led to Ganesh Mohalla. Then we got out of our taxi and walked into the lane. In less than a minute, we were joined by a few local men. 'Which book will you shoot, Dada?' they asked. (Why Bengalis started to refer to films as 'books' has remained a mystery to me. Why can't they call it a 'picture'?) Everyone wanted to watch the shooting. None of them had any idea how boring it could be, for very often it takes an hour to shoot a minute-long sequence. However, when their enthusiasm did not seem to

wane even after we explained this particular problem, we
decided to go along with their wishes since we needed their
help.

When we told them we were looking for someone who
could make an idol of Durga, they promptly said, 'Oh, you
should speak to Feluda.' At first we thought it was a joke, but
it turned out that there really was a potter called Feluda. He was
a shy and quiet man, no more than thirty-five years old. He
smiled and said, 'I am often teased about my name. Many
people here have read the stories of Feluda.'

We were naturally surprised to find that a local potter had
the same name as our hero, but I remembered other instances
in the past where I had been similarly surprised. When I came
to Varanasi to film *Aparajito*, I had met a boy called Anupam
whose pet name was Apu. A year later, I went to a place called
Neemtita to make *Jalsaghar* (The Music Room). I had to shoot
inside the house of the Chowdhurys, where I discovered that
one of their young servants was called Toofan. In the story of
Jalsaghar, the zamindar Vishwambhar Ray's favourite horse
was called Toofan. But that was not all. I had inspected several
other houses, but had been obliged to reject them all. When I
finally found this house in Neemtita, it seemed absolutely ideal.
Then I learnt that it was the very house where the original
zamindar, on whom the character of Vishwambhar was based,
had lived.

We met another potter that day called Bangshi Pal. The
potter in my story was called Shashi Pal. The similarity in these
names was just as startling.

*

We needed to look for two other things, apart from a potter.
These were, a hideout for the fraud sadhu, Machhli Baba; and

a suitable house for the Ghoshals, who owned the statue of Ganesh that got stolen.

We rose the next day half an hour before sunrise and took a taxi to Harishchandra Ghat. Then we began walking towards Dashashwamedh, going up and down great flights of stairs now and then to look at the houses at every ghat. By the time we reached Dashashwamedh, the sun was fairly high in the sky. Every ghat was teeming with bathers, particularly since it was makar sankranti, an auspicious day for bathing in the Ganges. There were quite a few hippies there, too; some were having tea, some strumming a sitar on the steps, and some had already begun smoking ganja. Several boats were floating down the river, packed with tourists from abroad. Many of them had movie cameras and seemed most anxious to capture this amazing spectacle.

Next to Dashashwamedh was Darbhanga Ghat. A steep flight of stairs led straight from the ghat to the front gate of the ancient palace of the Maharaja of Darbhanga. We went up the steps, by this time feeling tired as none of us was used to climbing so many steps. It seemed pretty extraordinary that dozens of old people, some even in their eighties, could go up and down these stairs several times every day, with perfect ease. There was a raised octagonal platform close to the ghat where pigeons were fed twice a day. Hundreds of pigeons came flying and settled on the ground. I had witnessed the same scene twenty-two years ago. Now, watching it once again, I got an idea how I could use it in my film.

The entrance to the palace was locked. We spoke to the chowkidar, but he said no one was allowed to go in. Yet, I could not come away without seeing the palace from inside. It was obvious that no one lived there now. So it could well act as a hideout for Machhli Baba.

Luckily, on being paid two rupees, the chowkidar brought

out a key and unlocked the door for us. My heart beat faster as
I stepped in, for I knew that there was no need to look any
further. I had got what I wanted. We must shoot in this
abandoned palace by the Ganges, and somehow, we must get
the necessary permission to do so. The palace was built at a
considerable height above the ghat. When we stood near the
railing of the passage that led from the front door to the main
building and looked down, the people at the ghat seemed quite
small. The noise, too, sounded faint from this distance. To the
north was a railway bridge, and to the south, the river curved
before the Ramnagar Fort and flowed eastward, vanishing into
the mist.

We crossed a second passage, went through an arch on the
right and entered the palace. Here, too, was an open courtyard;
a heap of broken old furniture had been dumped in a corner.

A dark staircase on our right went up to the first floor. I
had to switch on a torch—although it was broad daylight—to
find our way. A room upstairs proved ideal for Machhli Baba.
Seen through the camera, it would be obvious that no one ever
came here. Having made our choice, we came down again. On
our way out, we noticed a strange object. It was a lift. There
was no electricity to run it now, but when it was operational
during the time of the maharajas, it used to go up to the third
floor, where a Kali temple had been built. Presumably, all the
raja had to do on returning after bathing in the river was press
a button, and he was taken straight to the temple for his puja.

*

Machhli Baba's secret den was sorted out, and—
eventually—we got the necessary permission to shoot inside
the palace. Now we had to look for a house for the Ghoshals.
As it turned out, there were two suitable houses. The first was

in Memurganj, but we had to reject it. Although it fitted the description in the book, there was nothing visible from it to suggest that it was a house in Varanasi. We left it and went on to the second house that had been recommended.

This house was in Nagwa. The particular area in Nagwa where we had to go was called Lanka. The house used to belong to a Mr Gyan Chakravarty, the ex-Vice Chancellor of a university in UP. He had died some years ago. Now the house was the property of the Dalmias. A long driveway led from the front gate to the house, which was hidden behind a number of trees. It was a large mansion. No one lived there now. Its massive compound bore evidence of its past grandeur. Yes, this house would be most suitable for the Ghoshals in my film. The river was not far, but the plinth of the house was so high that even during the monsoon there was no fear of flooding. Apparently, the land had once belonged to an English lady. Soon after she came to know Gyan Chakravarty, she dreamt one night that he had been her own child in a previous life. Having lived in Varanasi for many years, this lady had been influenced by Hindu beliefs and had started to believe in reincarnations. The upshot was that, as a result of her dream, she left all the land and her other assets to Mr Chakravarty. The house was built almost fifty years ago, and Feluda's story was going to be filmed there, in 1978.

The most striking thing about the house was its roof. Quite a few scenes had to be shot here, since it was on the roof that little Ruku—the young hero of our film—had his playroom. There was, in fact, a room on the right as we came up the stairs that matched the description of Ruku's room in the book.

There was a remarkable view of the city of Varanasi from the roof. The river stretched beyond the railway bridge in the far distance, its banks spread out like the blade of a giant sickle. It was not possible to see much in the early morning mist; but as the sun rose higher, the mist cleared and virtually the whole city became visible. To the south of the house, all the land stretching up to the river-bank had belonged to Mr Chakravarty. Now, arhar daal and marigold were grown on that land. Most of the marigold used for Durga Puja came from here, we were told.

All of us felt very pleased with the house. What was even better was that getting the necessary permission to shoot here was no problem at all. We returned to Calcutta on the fourth day, relaxed and reassured. In the few days that we'd spend in Calcutta, we would have to look for a young boy to play Ruku. Our shooting would start from the thirteenth of February.

*

On this short visit to Varanasi, I was accompanied by four other people: our cameraman Soumendu, art director Ashok (who would have to rebuild the sets in Calcutta to match the buildings in Varanasi), my assistant Punu Sen and our production manager Anil Babu. It was Anil Babu's job to make sure we had the permission to shoot wherever we went, look after the whole unit, and keep an eye on expenses.

When we left again for Varanasi to shoot the film, there were twenty-three of us, barring coolies and labourers. We reserved a whole compartment and travelled together, as was our normal practice. Amongst the actors, only Feluda came with us, the others were required to be in Varanasi only the day before their presence was needed for our shooting. Anil Babu remained in Calcutta to ensure that these other actors caught the right train on the right day.

I have already mentioned that we had to find a suitable boy to play Ruku. This we achieved only a few hours before getting into the train that was going to take us from Howrah to Varanasi.

We had had to reject one boy whom we had seen earlier. Ruku, in the story, was seven years old. The boy we saw was eight but, when seen on the screen, he appeared to be ten. So we had to reject him, although he did quite well in the screen test.

It is often necessary to have a screen test before selecting a new actor. The actor is given a few lines of dialogue that suit the role he is going to play. He has to learn those lines and act in front of the camera, just as the director tells him. Then his acting is seen on the screen to judge whether he is the right choice for the role. It is not always possible to make this decision simply by watching a person. Usually, when a person talks, we don't stare unblinkingly at him, but the camera does precisely that. That is why it can pick up all the subtle weaknesses in one's acting. Equally, when an actor appears pretty ordinary, the camera can make him seem special by capturing his strengths, which one might miss otherwise.

We found ourselves in real trouble after being forced to reject the boy we had tested. Plenty of other boys came for more screen tests, but none of them seemed suitable. We were running out of time, the date for the shooting had been fixed, and train and hotel reservations made. Soon, the day of our departure dawned. We were to leave at night by the Doon Express. At around half past eleven in the morning, my assistant Punu rang me from Tollygunj, sounding very excited. Apparently, he had seen a boy outside a shop and followed him all the way to his house. Then he had spoken to the boy's mother, who had said that we were welcome to use her son in our film if we found him suitable. I told Punu to bring both the child and his mother to my house. They arrived in half an hour, and one look at Jit Bose and a few words with him told me that I had found the right Ruku.

This was not the first time I had found a young actor in a rather strange manner. As I have mentioned already, when I was making *Pather Panchali*, initially I had failed to find a small boy to play Apu. Ultimately, we found the right boy from the house next door.

For *Aparajito*, we needed a slightly older Apu. Once again, we saw several boys, but did not find any of them suitable. Then, one day, as I was returning from a village called Sonarpur, I saw a group of schoolboys get into the same railway compartment. They were coming back after a school excursion. One of the boys in that group struck me as eminently suitable for Apu, but in that crowded compartment I did not get the chance to talk to him. The train stopped at Ballygunj. The boys got off here with me and I saw that particular boy get into a tram. I ran to catch the same tram, found him, and went and sat beside him. Then I told him frankly what I wanted. He nodded and said yes immediately. 'How do you know your parents are not going to object?' I asked him. He then explained that he had no father, and he knew his mother would not object. He did not even have to ask her. As things turned out, he was right. I found the right Apu almost by accident; but, for the same film, we could not find a suitable woman to play the role of Apu's friend, Leela. Eventually, the character of Leela had to be dropped altogether.

By the time we left for Varanasi, the casting for *Joi Baba Felunath* was complete. Nearly all the actors had a few scenes in Varanasi. The rest would be shot in the studio in Calcutta between March and May. There was another actor travelling with us, apart from Soumitra Chatterjee (who played Feluda). This other actor had a job, in addition to acting, that was no less important or difficult. All of us knew that the alleys and the ghats of Varanasi were going to be crowded. There were two people in our unit who were experts at controlling crowds. One was Bhanu Ghosh, who could roar loudly enough to make people spring back, and the other was the actor, Kamu

Mukherjee (who had played the villain, Mandar Bose, in *Shonar Kella*). He had travelled with us by train before, more than once, when we went to film *Goopy Gyne* and *Shonar Kella* in Rajasthan. Every morning, as the train pulled in at a station, Kamu would wake us with a loud '*Jaago, Bangali!*' (Wake up, Bengalis!) One shout was usually enough to wake the whole troop. This was then followed by hot cups of tea, also arranged by Kamu. While shooting an important scene in the same film, it was Kamu who picked up an extremely poisonous scorpion, and held it between two fingers, deftly avoiding its sting. To tell you the truth, one can write a whole book on Kamu's antics. Let me narrate a few.

When we went to Rajasthan for the first time to make *Goopy Gyne Bagha Byne*, an actor called Rajkumar Lahiri travelled with us. He began buying naagras of various sizes and designs as soon as we entered Rajasthan. Apparently, his family had several members, and they had all asked him to bring them naagras. Mr Lahiri began tying these naagras with strings to form a bundle. By the time we reached Jaisalmer, it had acquired the size of a washerman's bundle. Everyone in the unit had noticed what Mr Lahiri was doing.

We stayed in the maharaja's guest house in Jaisalmer, called Jawahar Nivas. Mr Lahiri's room was next to mine on the first floor. Jawahar Nivas was really a small palace, made of yellow sandstone. Its rooms were big with very high ceilings. From every window, one could get a view of either the fort or the sandy desert.

Two days passed eventlessly. On the third day, as I was sitting in my room in the evening, working out our schedule for the next day, Mr Lahiri turned up. He cleared his throat, hesitated for a few moments, then said, 'Er . . . I have . . . er . . . a complaint.' This had to be important, or he would not have come straight to me. 'What is it, Mr Lahiri?' I asked him.

'I cannot find my naagras.'

'Not a single one?'

'No, not a single one. Perhaps, someone has . . . you know . . . done something.' I could see that Mr Lahiri was too embarrassed to suggest that the entire bundle have been stolen. 'Very well, let me see what I can do,' I told him as reassuringly as I could. He left, still looking distinctly worried and unhappy.

I began making enquiries, but no one could throw any light on this matter. Kamu came to me after everyone else had gone. My suspicions had already fallen on him. When I asked him straightaway if he knew anything about the stolen naagras, he seemed perfectly taken aback. 'Stolen?' he cried. 'Who said they have been stolen? They are in Mr Lahiri's room, safe and sound. Come with me, I will show you.'

I went with him into the next room. Kamu pointed at the ceiling. The bundle of naagras was hanging from a beam like a chandelier, directly over Mr Lahiri's bed. It was so high that no one could have noticed it easily.

'It was taking up such a lot of space on the floor that I thought getting it out of the way was a good idea,' Kamu explained. Then, seeing the look of total bewilderment on Mr Lahiri's face, he added, 'If I knew you would go and complain behind my back, do you know what I'd have done? I'd have waited until you'd gone to bed, then simply cut that string tied to the ceiling. Then you'd have seen what "Naagra Falls" can be like!'

There is something else about Kamu that deserves a special mention here. It is his ability to find strange but appropriate analogies. Once, my wife offered him a plate of biscuits when he came to visit us. Kamu took one bite from a biscuit and asked, 'Have you put silencers on these?' What he meant was that the biscuits had gone soft and soggy, and were not making crunchy noises while being chewed, as they should have done. During our stay in Jaisalmer, one day Kamu announced that the noise from a thresher had kept him awake all night. When we asked him where he had found a thresher in Jaisalmer, he pointed at the old actor, Govind Chakravarty, who was sharing a room with Kamu. Apparently, Mr Chakravarty had asthma, and in the early hours of the morning, he often had a fit of coughing. Anyone who has heard the noise from a thresher and the wheezy coughs of an asthmatic would realize how very appropriate Kamu's description was.

*

Upon reaching Varanasi, we spent the first two days re-inspecting all the chosen sites, and hiring a houseboat (called a *baujra*, and not unlike the houseboats in Srinagar). This boat would be the villain Maganlal's private boat, and on the days when it was not needed for our shooting, it could carry our equipment from one ghat to another. A large boat was hired for this purpose, as well as a team of workmen to give it a fresh coat of paint and draw pictures on it. By its door were painted a couple of armed guards, and around the windows creepers with flowers. Many houses in Varanasi have pictures on their front walls—elephants, horses, peacocks, parrots, tigers, kings and soldiers. These are usually drawn when there is a wedding in a family. Twenty years ago, I had noticed that each picture had the touch of a master painter. Now, it was no longer possible to find someone really good and talented without having to search pretty widely.

We reached Darbhanga Ghat on the first day of shooting (13 February) at half past six in the morning. Every scene leading up to the discovery of Machhli Baba's den was filmed in the next four hours. Those who make films know that if three minutes' worth is shot in a day, then that is pretty good going.

By that I mean scenes that would take three minutes to show on
the screen. It usually takes forty to forty-five days to complete
a film that runs for two hours (120 minutes). If one is working
in a studio, it is possible to get three minutes of shots, by
working consistently for eight hours. Working outdoors is
much more difficult. Today, however, we had created a record
by taking enough shots that would run for nearly five minutes.

Since this was our first day, there were not too many people
crowding the ghat. Those who had come forward to watch us
at work were used in the film as part of the background. There
is no end to the variety of people who visit the ghats of Varanasi,
but for our film we needed those who were particularly suitable.
So we had to keep an eye out for sadhus in saffron clothes,
pandas, pilgrims, or old women with bent backs, leaning
heavily on sticks. The minute we saw any of them, we had to
speak to them and see if they'd agree to be a part of our shot.
Even cows and goats and dogs roaming freely in the ghat were
used in our film. If we had so wished, we could have sought
help from the local police and filmed each scene in a totally
empty ghat. But to show Feluda as the only person in a ghat in
Varanasi, without another soul in sight, would hardly have been
realistic. So we had to go to a lot of trouble to get just the right
sort of people in the background.

The broken furniture we had seen in the courtyard inside
the Darbhanga Palace had been transferred to the first floor,
near the room chosen for Machhli Baba. When Feluda is seen
snooping in there and as the man returns unexpectedly, all that
furniture acts as a screen behind which Feluda can duck quickly.

We finished the morning's shooting and returned to our
hotel by half past eleven. In the evening, we had to return to the
same ghat at four o'clock, to film the scene in which Maganlal
arrives in his boat to have a darshan of Machhli Baba.

*

We went back to the ghat as planned, but saw to our dismay that the relatively empty ghat where we had worked only that morning was now looking like a football stadium. Even on the river, the number of boats had increased considerably. Those who could not find any room on the steps of the ghat obviously thought they could watch the tamasha from the river. To tell the truth, the boats did not seem out of place for many people who come on holiday to Varanasi take a boat in the evening for a cruise down the river. It was the crowd at the ghat that worried us. Let me give you an example from an earlier film I had made, just to show you how dangerous it can be when a vast number of people turn up to watch a shooting.

The outdoor scenes in the film *Chiriakhana* (The Zoo) were shot in a village called Bamungachhi near Calcutta. In a large open space in the middle of a mango orchard, we had built the sets of Golap Colony, surrounded by a compound wall. In the story, a retired judge had built this colony. It had a nursery, a pond, about six cottages for the residents of the colony, a bungalow for the judge himself, around ten cowsheds and chicken coops, protected by a fence. The place where the set was being built was very quiet, so the construction could go ahead peacefully, even if it meant a lot of hard work. It took us nearly a month to have everything ready. Then the shooting began. It was expected to go on for another month.

The local railway station was a couple of miles away from our Golap Colony. Occasionally, we could hear a train come and go. It was generally known that a train from Calcutta arrived every day in the afternoon.

No one disturbed us in the first few days. Then, one day, the departure of the afternoon train from Calcutta was followed by a noise in the distance. It sounded as if a lot of people were

shouting together. Gradually, as the noise got louder, we
realized a group of boys was walking in our direction, shouting
slogans, 'We must be allowed to see the shooting! Inquilab
zindabad!' Then they came closer still, and we could suddenly
see the pointed end of spears across the wall. Good heavens,
were they armed? It turned out eventually that what we had seen
were not spears, but about fifty sugarcanes that the boys had
collected from a field on their way. The first thing they did on
reaching our colony was climb all the mango trees that were
left standing outside the compound wall. To our amazement,
we saw that the leaves on those trees were practically hidden
by the bodies that were now settled on their branches. At first,
we made an attempt to make them see reason, but they
responded to our appeal by pelting us with stones. After that,
there did not seem to be any point in making further attempts,
so we began our work. However, only an hour later, our work
was brought to a halt by a loud crash, which was followed
almost immediately by yells and screams.

A branch on which seven boys were sitting had given way
and crashed to the ground. One of the boys appeared to be
seriously injured. One of our own actors, Shubhendu
Chattopadhyay, had to give him first aid. Shubhendu had once
been a medical student.

Strangely enough, even after such a disaster, no one
seemed to have lost their enthusiasm. All the other boys
continued to sit on the trees. We had to carry on with our
shooting like this for the next four days. What was most
amazing was that even ladies turned up to join the audience. I
actually saw some of the boys helping middle-aged ladies get
on to a branch. The women, delighted at this golden
opportunity, spent hour after hour in treetops without any
apparent discomfort. The truth of the matter is that most people
forget pretty often that a film has to be seen on the screen. They

think the shooting of a film is something like a play or a spectacle, that can be watched in an open field.

Anyway, going back to what happened in Varanasi, we knew there would be a lot of people at the ghats, so we had brought thick ropes. Bhanu and Kamu took those out and began cordoning off the area where the main action was going to take place. We had to be very careful not to sound impatient or impolite. It had to be explained to everyone, calmly and politely, how badly our work would suffer if they pressed forward. However, people seemed to listen only when we declared that unless they stayed out of the way, we would pack up and go home. If we did that, obviously there would not be anything left for them to see. Once this announcement was made, everyone stepped back and remained behind the cordon.

While we were dealing with the crowd, Utpal Dutt (who was playing the role of Maganlal Meghraj) had got into his boat and was waiting at another ghat. One of our men was there with him. When we were ready, we would signal to him and the boat would start coming towards our ghat. Feluda, Lalmohan Babu and Topshe were waiting at Darbhanga Ghat, together with Satya Bandopadhyay, who was playing Niranjan Chakravarty, the manager of the guest house where they were staying. He would spot Maganlal's boat, and point him out to Feluda, who would then peer through his binoculars to get a closer look. Then the boat would pull up at our ghat and Maganlal would climb down from its roof, pick up a silver plate covered with a silk handkerchief from one of his servants, and make his way to Machhli Baba to offer it as a gift. Maganlal, it was said, was among the most devoted followers of the Baba. He would pass Feluda on his way.

Although Machhli Baba was supposed to be holding a discourse in one corner of Darbhanga Ghat, we were going to film the following action-packed sequence in a studio as that would be a lot more convenient. At this moment, in February, we simply shot the scene of Maganlal's arrival. In April, in Calcutta, we were going to show him reaching Machhli Baba and handing him the silver plate. People who saw the film would never be able to guess the time difference between the two scenes.

On the first day, the scene that was shot was one of the very early scenes in the film. On the second day, we shot a scene that features towards the end of the film. It was, in some ways, a similar scene in that it showed Maganlal arrive in his boat and climb the steps of the ghat with another gift in his hand. But, this time, he was being watched only by Topshe and Lalmohan Babu. Both were in disguise. Feluda had told them to dress as sadhus. So they were wearing saffron robes, had long matted hair, sandalwood marks on their foreheads and rudraksha beads round their necks. Lalmohan Babu even had a copper pot and a staff in his hands. He was trying to give his disguise an authentic touch by chanting mantras occasionally, but Topshe was keeping a careful eye on him to make sure he did not overdo it. We realized what a terrific job our make-up man had done, when a panda gave Lalmohan Babu a deep bow with folded hands the minute he reached the ghat. Lalmohan Babu looked at the man through half-closed eyes and blessed him with cool nonchalance.

In spite of the crowd, we managed to film this scene with remarkable ease. When we had finished, most of us got into the boat instead of trying to fight our way through hundreds of people. The boat then took us to Dashashwamedh Ghat. We decided to have our lunch on the river. In fact, this became a regular practice when we had to spend the whole day working at the ghats. We would get packed lunches and have a meal in the boat. The used cartons would be thrown out of the window, to be pounced on by crows and kites for any scraps of meat they could find.

*

We finished shooting at Darbhanga and moved to Kedar Ghat, which was some distance away. No one knew we were going to a different ghat, so when we arrived at Kedar in the evening, we found it empty. However, the news spread amazingly quickly, and before we knew it, thousands of people were walking towards Kedar. We prepared for battle once more.

Fortunately, this time the crowd did not try breaking through the cordon. But some of the shots involved funny actions by Lalmohan Babu, which made the audience burst into laughter. The sound of laughter drowned the lines spoken by the actors on our tape recorder. How were we going to hear exactly what the actors were saying, if the audience wiped out every other sound by laughing so loudly? Yet, we simply had to record the dialogue being spoken, for when we returned to Calcutta, the three actors would have to hear the same tape and speak the same lines in exactly the same way. If they could do this successfully, the spoken words would match their lip movements after the shots were taken. This business of recording the dialogues in a studio is called 'dubbing'.

In spite of all these problems, we finished shooting at the ghat. It was now time to turn our attention to the alleys. Feluda and the others were staying at the Calcutta Lodge near Dashashwamedh Ghat. They were to be shown going through the lane leading out of the Vishwanath temple, past Gyan Bapi Masjid, and through a few more lanes before they reached Maghanlal's house. There were a few lines of dialogue in these shots, and a scene where Lalmohan Babu is both startled and frightened by the appearance of a bull. We managed to finish our work near the temple and Gyan Bapi, and proceeded to the lane where the trio were supposed to find the bull. When I had written the screenplay in Calcutta, I had no idea that the number of bulls in Varanasi had diminished. But I could not imagine the streets of Varanasi without bulls, or my film without that scene showing Lalmohan Babu's confrontation with one. The local people said there were no bulls in the vicinity. If we wanted one, we would have to get it from the nearest ghat, which was a mile away. Not only did it mean travelling all that way, but there was no guarantee that a bull would be good enough to leave its own area and amble down to where we wanted it.

Kamu volunteered to help. He said he would take a few bundles of spinach and other vegetables to entice a bull and somehow get it to follow him to our lane. This seemed like a good idea. So Kamu left with good wishes from us all, and we settled down for a long wait. We had had to leave very early in the morning without any breakfast. Someone pointed out fresh jalebis being fried at a nearby stall. We had breakfast there.

Lalmohan Babu, I noticed, was looking thoughtful. Perhaps he was worried about his shot with the bull. Earlier, while shooting for *Shonar Kella*, he had had to tackle a camel. On that occasion, too, there had been reason for concern. But a camel is certainly a lot less ferocious than a bull. Its behaviour is so totally unpredictable.

This reminds me of another actor who had been extremely worried during the shooting of *Shonar Kella*. There was a scene where the villain, Mandar Bose, pushes a man called Dr Hajra off a cliff. Sailen Mukherjee was playing Dr Hajra. He knew what the scene involved, but I had not told him how the shot was going to be taken. What he did know was that Satyajit Ray liked things to be realistic. So he assumed that there was a strong possibility of being asked to jump off a cliff. When he left for

Rajasthan, he told his family, 'Don't be surprised if I return with a lot of broken bones.' It was not until we reached Jaipur and it was time to take the shot that Sailen learnt what was going to happen. Mandar Bose would certainly give him a push, but Bhanu would stand at an appropriate spot to catch him before he rolled down the hill. The next shot would show him lying injured at the bottom of the hill. So there was no need for him to worry. When these shots were over, Sailen rang up his family and said, 'It's all right, I am still in one piece!'

Back in Varanasi, a crowd had started to gather even in this little lane. The ghats had been full of Bengalis, but here there were mostly Hindi speakers. Nevertheless, they seemed just as keen to watch a film being made. If Kamu did find a bull, I wondered how he was going to bring it to us through so many people. Nearly an hour later, Kamu returned, alone. Hey, where was our bull? With a long face, Kamu explained what had happened. Apparently, a bull had indeed started to follow him, just as he had planned, but halfway through its journey, it had changed its mind and gone back to the ghat. So what could we do now? Leave the whole episode out? Impossible!

Suddenly, there was a commotion near the entrance to the alley. It had become generally known that we were looking for a bull. One of the local men had found one of rather impressive proportions. He had even found its owner. This was splendid news, but there was a problem. An iron railing stood at the entrance to the lane, coming between the bull and our camera. A medium-sized cow might have passed through it, but a bull of that size most certainly could not. There was no railing at the other end of the lane, but in order to get there, the bull would have to be persuaded to turn around and walk through four other lanes. There was no guarantee that this one would not change its mind too if it was made to walk that way. There was really one thing we could do. We took the camera to the other side of the railing.

The scene went like this: Feluda, Topshe and another man in a blue shirt (planted there by the villain, Maganlal) would pass the bull and walk on. Then Feluda would stop and turn back to find Lalmohan Babu hesitating. On being asked why he had stopped, Lalmohan Babu would explain that an astrologer had told him he would be in grave danger in 1978. He thought this bull signified that unspoken danger. At this, Feluda would tell him not to be silly, and Lalmohan Babu would somehow gather enough courage to walk past the huge bull and then sigh with relief.

After having found a suitable spot to place the camera, we had only just started to prepare for a rehearsal, when an angry hum rose from the audience. A cow or a bull was considered a holy animal. Many among those present thought we had no right to keep it captive in a small alley. There was obviously no time for a rehearsal. I said a short prayer and started the camera. Feluda, Topshe and the man in the blue shirt began walking as soon as I shouted, 'Action!' The third man was a local, so he was quite used to dealing with bulls. He walked past it nonchalantly, even prodding it a little to get it partly out of the way. Feluda and Topshe followed. Lalmohan Babu was supposed to stop several feet away from the animal. He did, just as the script said. But, at this moment, the bull suddenly turned around and shook its horns so violently at him that Lalmohan Babu nearly jumped out of his skin. The fear in his eyes was very real, he had to make no effort to 'act'. As a result of this, the shot turned out to be much more interesting than I had anticipated. Sadly, though, we discovered later that the camera had failed to work properly. So that beautiful shot with the bull could not be used after all. In the end, we had to get a cow to film the scene.

Sometimes in a film, the scenes that appear perfectly natural and easy can cause quite a lot of headache to the director and his crew to shoot. *Joi Baba Felunath* was no exception. Let me give you an example.

The first scene was supposed to show Feluda in one cycle rickshaw, and Topshe and Lalmohan Babu in another, travelling with all their luggage to Calcutta Lodge where they were going to stay. Showing them in long shots was no problem. But the audience would not be happy with that, particularly in the first scene. Moreover, a close shot would help establish the characters, and show their individual characteristics. Lalmohan Babu, for instance, could be shown raising his hands to touch his forehead each time his rickshaw passed a temple. This would indicate a sudden arousal of religious fervour in his heart, just because he was in a holy place.

The problem with a close-up was that such a shot could not be taken unless the camera was placed on the driver's seat. Obviously, if the driver's seat was occupied by the camera, there would be no one to drive the rickshaw! After much racking of brains, we hit upon a solution. If the driver's seat and the front wheel of the rickshaw could be removed altogether and the passenger's seat attached to the rear of a taxi, the cameraman could sit in the boot with the camera, and the taxi could pull the rickshaw, moving slowly at about the same speed as a rickshaw.

We spoke to some rickshaw-walas and one of them agreed to perform this surgical operation on his vehicle. His seat was detached, and the rear of the rickshaw was then tied with a rope to one of the three taxis we had hired. Someone removed the lid of the boot and we put our camera in it, tying it also with a rope. But then we realized that it was too close to the actors who were sitting in the passenger's seat. Since the passengers could not move back further, the camera had to. So, the surgical feat was carried a step further, and the glass behind the back seat of the taxi was removed. The camera was placed on the back seat. Now, on looking through it, I found that I had finally got what I wanted.

While these preparations were being made, as always a crowd had gathered around us. When our taxi started and I began taking the first shot, I saw that quite a few young men—possibly local hooligans—were cycling along right behind Topshe and Lalmohan Babu, in the hope that by doing so, they would get to appear in a film. With men like these, politeness was a waste of time. So the remaining members of our team joined us in trying to get rid of these camera-hoggers. We had to travel for a whole mile before we could finally get rid of the last one. Then, when I could be sure that we only had normal traffic and pedestrians around us, I shouted to the two actors from the taxi and told them the actual shooting was now going to start. After Topshe and Lalmohan Babu, Feluda sat in the same rickshaw, and we took a few shots with him. Those who do not know about the half-rickshaw and the towing taxi would never be able to guess how this whole sequence was filmed.

While we were in Varanasi, we shot only one scene at night. Everything else was filmed in daylight because shooting at night would have been much more difficult and complicated. To start with, we would have had to arrange enough lights. The bright lights attached to iron stands that are used in studios would have had to be carried everywhere. Not only would this have added to our luggage, it would have also meant making arrangements for extra electric connections wherever we went. If a particular area had no electricity at all, we would have had to use a generator. In other words, no matter where we worked at night, the local residents would have been disturbed and quite possibly annoyed. The only shots we took at night in Varanasi were taken in an area called Pandey Haveli.

Before I talk about this experience, perhaps I ought to mention another instance of night shooting. On that occasion, we were in Rajasthan, making *Shonar Kella*. The scene that was to be shot involved a train arriving at a small station in the middle of the night. We filmed the whole sequence on a dark and bitterly cold night.

Feluda, Lalmohan Babu and Topshe were going to get into the train bound for Jaisalmer at a station called Ramdeora. A few minutes after the train started, the villain Mandar Bose (played by Kamu Mukherjee); dressed as a Rajasthani, would climb into their compartment. The following action was going to be shot in a studio. But the action that took place outside the compartment had to be filmed on location. The most difficult shot was going to be the one that showed Mandar Bose hanging from a metal rod as he moved—extremely dangerously—from one compartment to another. Had this been a Hollywood film, we would have used a professional stuntman. Unfortunately, there are hardly any good stuntmen in Bengal. We had realized this years ago while making *Jalsaghar*. The last scene in this film showed the protagonist, zamindar Vishwambhar Ray, falling off a horse. We could hardly ask the leading actor, Chhabi Biswas, to do this himself. So, one of the best-known stuntmen of Calcutta, called Khan Sahib, was hired for the job. He did fall off the horse as required, but then he had to spend the next three days in bed. For this particular scene in *Shonar Kella*, Kamu had quite willingly volunteered to swing from the door of one compartment and jump to the next in a moving train. I knew what a daredevil he was, so I had every faith in him.

We had selected a small station called Lathi to shoot these scenes at night. A special train was at our disposal. Its driver had been briefed. He knew that he might be asked to move the train backwards and forwards.

There was another thing that we were going to have to use. This was a trolley, which was going to be pushed on a second railway track that ran parallel to the one on which our train stood. The camera was to be mounted on top of this trolley, and two railway coolies would push the trolley up and down the track. But that was not all. We had another camera, which was going to be handled by assistant cameraman Purnendu. He was required to climb on the roof of a compartment, lie on his stomach, and hold the camera in such a way that Mandar Bose's actions could be seen from above his head. This would make his acrobatics seem much more exciting.

By the time we were ready to take the first shot, it was midnight. The station was in the middle of the desert. Kamu got ready, climbed the steps that led to a compartment and grabbed a metal rod. But he snatched back his hand instantly, as if he had received an electric shock. The rod was so cold that it was impossible to hold it. It took him about five minutes to get used to the cold metal. Then, when he was ready once more, we shone a torch in the direction of the engine to tell the driver to start the train.

The coolies started pushing the trolley as soon as the train began moving. We would take the first shot when the train had gathered a little speed. My cameraman Soumendu and I were sitting on the trolley; Purnendu was up on the roof of a carriage, ready with his own camera; and the coolies were pushing our trolley with amazing skill, matching the speed with which the train was moving. The trolley was also being used to throw adequate light on Mandar Bose, without which he could hardly be seen.

We had to wait for a whole minute before the time seemed right to take the shot. So far, Kamu had been hanging from a door like a bat. Now, on being given a signal, he swung himself from one door to another, very much like a trapeze artiste in a circus, and we got a perfect shot without having to do a single retake.

This particular scene was shot at a time and place where there was no question of a gawking audience. We could therefore finish our work quickly and peacefully. In Varanasi, we had decided to start shooting in a little lane in Pandey Haveli at eight p.m. Feluda and the others were out for a walk after dinner. The shot was going to be chiefly Lalmohan Babu's, for he wanted a taste of the atmosphere in Varanasi late at night, in the hope that it would give him new ideas for his next novel. They were to be shown chatting and walking down a totally empty lane, rather eerie in its silence. In the next lane, at the same time, a gruesome murder would take place.

We had calculated how much time the trio were going to take to finish speaking the lines written for them. With this in view, three lanes in Pandey Haveli had been selected. Feluda and the others would have to stroll down all three. We had noticed that these lanes were rather poorly lit, so we needed to bring our own lights. It was decided that the electricians would get there by six o'clock to set the lights up. We would arrive a couple of hours later.

An astounding spectacle awaited us when we got there at eight o'clock. There was a relatively large area between two of the lanes we had chosen. Nearly a thousand people had collected there—young and old, male and female, Bengalis as well as non-Bengalis. There wasn't even enough room for us to set up our equipment to start shooting. Every single person was standing as if rooted to the ground. No one appeared to have the sense to realize that unless they moved away, there was no question of any shooting at all.

Now I had to raise my voice (since the people in the crowd were not exactly waiting in silence). Assisted by a few other men from the team, I yelled and told them that there would be no shooting unless the crowd dispersed. This warning was repeated at least five times, but it fell on deaf ears. Eventually, I told my crew to pack up and return to the hotel. Clearly, the only thing we could do was build an appropriate studio set in Calcutta to recreate the alleys of Varanasi. There was no way we could shoot here.

We went back to our hotel, had our dinner and were preparing to go to bed, when suddenly the doorbell rang. I opened the door of my room to find two young men. It turned out that they were residents of Pandey Haveli. They had come to offer profuse apologies and make an appeal. 'Please, sir, give us another chance,' they said. 'If you come back tomorrow a little later than eight o'clock, we guarantee there won't be any problem. If you go back without being able to work in our area, we'll get a bad name . . . and that will leave a permanent mark on the city's reputation!'

I thought things over and agreed to give it another go. 'Very well,' I said. 'But if we see even a small crowd, we'll return at once!'

We went back the following night at eleven o'clock. None of us had really expected those two men to keep their word. But, to our amazement, we found the streets empty. We were allowed to work perfectly undisturbed. By the time we finished, it was three in the morning. Even in a studio, it would not have been possible to work so peacefully.

The only thing that caused a minor problem was the enthusiasm of a local shop called Rinku Silk House. Having heard that a film was going to be shot in these lanes, they had pasted posters all over the place. No matter where we looked—on the walls of houses and temples, gates and lamposts—there was a poster enjoining everyone to visit Rinku Silk House. The owner of the shop happened to be present, so we explained to him that if those posters were allowed to remain, there was a strong possibility that our audience would pay more attention to his posters than the actions of Feluda & Co. While that might help his business, it would cause our film quite a lot of damage, and this we could not allow. The man looked a bit crestfallen at this, but Bhanu and some of the others soon removed virtually all the posters, leaving only a couple in discreet corners.

Then we had to turn our attention to recording the sound. Normally, although the lines spoken by actors are recorded during outdoor shooting, what is recorded on location cannot be used in the film for there are always other noises that disturb the dialogues. So the recorded sound is used as a 'guide-track'. The actors hear this guide-track later in the silence of a studio and the same lines are dubbed.

There was a slight problem in the scene that we were now going to shoot. Feluda, Topshe and Lalmohan Babu were going to be shown from a distance, walking down an alley, speaking every now and then. If the sound recordist moved with them to capture their lines, the camera would pick him up too.

We got round this problem by giving Lalmohan Babu a shoulder bag. In the bag was a small tape recorder. It was switched on just before a shot was taken. After the shot, it was played back to make sure the sound was clear enough. Needless to say, though the bag was slung from Lalmohan Babu's shoulder, the tape recorder caught the lines spoken by all three.

*

We spent thirteen days in Varanasi. In that time, we managed to shoot—on average—enough scenes that would run for three minutes on the screen every day. That meant one-third of the film was complete when we returned to Calcutta.

Please, Please, Bagh Mama

Years after *Goopy Gyne Bagha Byne* was released I decided to film the sequel to it, *Hirak Rajar Deshey* (The Kingdom of Diamonds). Goopy and Bagha embark on more adventures in this film when they happen to arrive at a country ruled by the evil and tyrannical Hirak Raja (the Diamond king). In Hirak Raja's treasury, there is a chest full of diamonds. Goopy and Bagha have to steal a number of these, for they need to bribe the royal guards. The wicked king has to be removed. It will be easy to get rid of him if his guards can be bought off. This is a plan the local teacher, Udayan Pundit, has come up with. Goopy and Bagha have joined hands with him to put an end to the king's tyranny.

The duo arrive at the treasury. The door has a guard pacing up and down. But Goopy has been given a boon by the king of ghosts. When he sings, no one can move an inch, or speak a word. So he now starts singing, and it becomes very easy for Bagha to tie the hands and feet of the guard with thick ropes, gag his mouth, and take the key from him. They then unlock the huge padlock on the door and step in, thinking happily that there are no more obstacles in their way. How are they to know that a tiger is sitting inside, to guard the keys to the three padlocks that are placed on the chest? If Goopy can sing, the tiger will be mesmerized, too. But Goopy himself is stunned and his throat goes totally dry. How is he to sing?

He tries very hard and, at last, manages to get a few words out:

Please, please, Bagh Mama (Uncle Tiger)
Do not be cross, Mama,
Who knew you were there in this room?

The charm works. The tiger sits quietly, without moving. Bagha inches forward, leans over the animal, and takes the key-ring with the three keys. After that, it is simply a matter of opening the chest and helping himself to the diamonds.

This was the scene that had to be shot. Those of you who have seen *Hirak Rajar Deshey* (The Kingdom of Diamonds) would have seen it on the screen. Let me now tell you how we did it.

Many Hindi films nowadays use tigers and lions. Most of these animals come from Madras. All reputed circuses these days are from South India. So we decided to shoot this scene with the tiger in a studio in Madras. Ten years ago, when making *Goopy Gyne Bagha Byne*, we had had to take a tiger to a village and shoot a scene in a bamboo grove. That was a memorable experience. This time, too, we had a remarkable experience, of a different kind.

A Bengali gentleman, who lived in Madras, had been asked to make enquiries about hiring a tiger. He had contacts in the film world, and was generally known as being helpful to all those who went from Bengal to shoot a film in Madras. There might be trouble if I use his real name, so I am going to call him Mr B. Mr B wanted to know the details of the scene that involved the tiger. We told him. Then he asked us to send him a tape with Goopy's song on it. If it was played to the tiger a number of times, that might help. Normally, all songs are recorded before the shooting of a film begins. We had no problem in sending a cassette to Madras, with the song 'Please, please, Bagh Mama' on it.

Ten days before the shooting was to start, Ashok Bose from our unit left for Madras to start working in a studio called Prasad. His job was to build a set showing the treasury. Usually, wooden frames are used to build sets in studios. When these are covered with plaster, they look quite solid, really no different from the real thing made with bricks and cement. Only if you tap the structure does it makes a hollow sound.

It was decided that the tiger would wait in a room adjacent to the treasury. Between the two rooms, there would be an arch. Above the tiger, on the wall, would be a nail from which would hang the key-ring.

We reached Madras two days before the shooting started. All of us were anxious to see the tiger. The whole scene would be spoilt if the animal did not look powerful and ferocious enough. No matter what Mr B kept telling us, none of us could really relax until we had seen it for ourselves. So we went with Mr B the next morning to visit the tiger. There were other animals, too. Under a shelter, there was a baby elephant, rocking to and fro. Mr B had taken a bunch of bananas with him. He began feeding these to the elephant, one by one. Why was he doing this? Surely we were here to look at a tiger, not an elephant? It turned out that the trainer of the tiger had gone out, but was expected soon.

When the trainer arrived, we were taken to a room where the tiger was shut in its cage. It was the same tiger, we were told, that had heard the song taped on our cassette, time and time again. It was quite ready to shoot the scene.

The room was dark. It was not possible to see the tiger very clearly. I felt dissatisfied, and asked the trainer: 'Can't you bring it outside?'

'Sure.'

'Then that's what we'd like you to do, please. We want to see it in the open, not inside a room.'

For some reason, the trainer seemed strangely reluctant to do as he was told. Mr B, too, seemed to stiffen at my words. What was going on?

It did not take us long to find out. As soon as the tiger emerged from its cage and appeared out in the open, we could see that it was old; its days of ferocity were long over. To tell the truth, I had never seen such a doddering, cantakerous old tiger outside a village circus. Its eyes were dim; it had even begun to lose the hair on its body. It snarled and growled the instant it was released, registering its protest through a series of weird noises. Was this tiger going to guard the chest in the royal treasury? Impossible!

I looked at Mr B. He was standing there, looking profoundly guilty. 'Do you mean to say this is the only well-trained tiger in Madras?' I asked. Mr B nodded. This tiger had heard the relevant song, and its trainer had been paid an advance of two thousand rupees. The total budget of a film often amounts to a million rupees or more. Two thousand was perhaps not a vast sum. But that was not the point. The point was that we had gone all the way to Madras, every other arrangement to start shooting was complete, the sets were ready, we were supposed to start our work the next day, but we had not yet found a suitable tiger. What were we going to do?

I found one thing most puzzling. The animals I had seen in Hindi films had all been healthy and strong. I knew that they had come from Madras. Where had they gone? Mr B could not give me an answer. All he could do was mutter, 'This is the best!'

We returned to our hotel deeply worried. Mr B had to be told, in no uncertain terms, that unless he could find a better tiger by that evening, there would be hell to pay.

When I went to the studio in the evening, I was in a state close to panic. I could feel that all our plans were going to be ruined. Either the scene with the tiger would have to be dropped, or—worse than that—we would somehow have to manage with the mangy old tiger we had seen in the morning.

Within a few minutes of my reaching the studio, Mr B swept in. He had been able to contact another trainer, he said, who had a very good tiger. It would be available for a day's shooting the next day. The trainer did not live very far away.

I got into a car and left with Mr B, who sat giving directions to the driver. Only a minute later, he said, 'Here we are!'

It was impossible to tell from the outside that a trainer lived here with several wild animals. Quite close to the road was an open area, covered by tin sheets. The trainer's house was just behind it. But we did not have to go that far. Only a short walk from the car brought us to a cage on our left. It contained a leopard. It was followed by three more cages, each kept close to the other. There was a second leopard in one. The other two had a lion and a tiger.

One look at the tiger removed all my anxieties, and I could breathe easy again. Who knew I would find exactly what I was looking for in a dingy little place like this? This animal truly had a regal air about it—its appearance was a treat for the eyes.

The trainer was equally impressive. His name was Tiger Govindarajan. Every supplier of tigers in Madras likes adding the word 'Tiger' before his name. Govindarajan was originally from Rajasthan, but he had lived in Madras for many years, and changed his name to a Tamil one. He was once involved with circuses. Now he was in the business of supplying animals for film-making. He told us that he had married five times. The woman he currently lived with was his wife number five. Both trained animals.

'What would you like my tiger to do?' asked Tiger

Govindarajan.

'It's quite simple,' I replied. 'One of our actors will sing. The tiger only has to sit in a corner quietly and hear the song. That's all.'

Govindarajan shook his head morosely. 'If you tell the pilot of a jet to drive a bullock cart, do you think he can? My tiger's a fighter. It's fought with so many big stars from Bombay. How do you expect it to simply sit quietly in a corner?'

Oh God, here was a fresh problem. 'Bring your tiger to the studio, anyway,' we told him. 'Then we'll see what we can do.'

At this, the trainer relented. Perhaps our words had made him feel a little sorry. 'All right,' he said. 'The tiger won't need any special training from me. My wife alone will be able to manage.'

The scene with the tiger in *Goopy Gyne Bagha Byne* did not require Goopy or Bagha—or anyone else—to go anywhere near the tiger. It had remained in a bamboo grove, at least forty or fifty feet away from the actors. Moreover, it was wearing a collar, to which was tied a strong wire. Its trainer was holding one end of it. This time, things would have to be different.

We would have to place the camera quite close to the tiger. It could not wear a collar this time. If it did, it might become obvious that the tiger was tied to a wire. That would be awful. Besides, Bagha would have to stand really close to the tiger to collect the key-ring.

When using a wild animal in a film, it is customary to give the animal a sedative of some kind. We decided to do the same. If we could have complete faith in the trainer, the use of drugs might not have been necessary. However, Govindarajan's behaviour did not inspire a great deal of confidence. Perhaps I should mention here that even when drugs are administered their effects do not last for very long. I realized this while shooting this scene. We learnt that day what a difficult job it is to keep a tiger—sedated or otherwise—sitting quietly in a corner.

We reached the studio the next day at nine. The tiger was expected at ten o'clock. It arrived on time in its special cage, which was placed on a truck. The cage had wheels. It was taken off the truck, and pushed to stand at the entrance to the treasury. Then the tiger was released, so that it could go straight into the next room where it was supposed to sit. It was accompanied by the trainer's wife and another young man, who looked as if he was quite used to dealing with the animal. Mr Govindarajan himself climbed a high platform about fifteen feet away to watch the proceedings. It is very difficult to describe the emotions of each member of the unit. All of us had to keep calm and pretend we did not care. So what if there was a tiger in the studio? But, speaking for myself, I can tell you now that even if one might not actually feel afraid, the presence of a tiger outside its cage, at such close proximity, automatically makes one's pulse run faster.

The actor, Robi Ghosh, was playing the role of Bagha. Today was sure to be a memorable day in his life, for what was going to be put to the test would not simply be his acting skills, but also his courage. It was he who was supposed to get really close to the tiger.

We decided to first take those shots in which the tiger appears alone. The camera was placed about fifteen feet away from the animal. I peered through it, waiting patiently. It was switched on the minute the tiger stopped being restless and looked in our direction. It kept running for as long as he remained still. The best shots from these would be selected eventually, and inserted between the lines of Goopy's song, to make it seem as if the tiger was listening to it intently.

After about an hour, I noticed something I had never seen before. Thanks to the warm climate in Madras and the heat